IMAGES OF WAR

BATTLE OF PELELIU 1944:

THREE DAYS THAT TURNED INTO THREE MONTHS

RARE PHOTOGRAPHS FROM WARTIME ARCHIVES

IMAGES OF WAR
BATTLE OF PELELIU 1944:
THREE DAYS THAT TURNED INTO THREE MONTHS

RARE PHOTOGRAPHS FROM WARTIME ARCHIVES

JIM MORAN

FRONTLINE BOOKS

First published in Great Britain in 2022 by
FRONTLINE BOOKS
An imprint of
Pen & Sword Books Ltd
Yorkshire – Philadelphia

Copyright © Jim Moran 2022

ISBN 978 1 52677 821 5

A CIP catalogue record for this book is
available from the British Library.

Printed and bound in India by Replika Press Pvt. Ltd.

Pen & Sword Books Limited incorporates the imprints of Atlas, Archaeology, Aviation,
Discovery, Family History, Fiction, History, Maritime, Military, Military Classics, Politics,
Select, Transport, True Crime, Air World, Frontline Publishing, Leo Cooper, Remember
When, Seaforth Publishing, The Praetorian Press, Wharncliffe Local History, Wharncliffe
Transport, Wharncliffe True Crime and White Owl.

For a complete list of Pen & Sword titles please contact

PEN & SWORD BOOKS LIMITED
47 Church Street, Barnsley, South Yorkshire, S70 2AS, England
E-mail: enquiries@pen-and-sword.co.uk
Website: www.pen-and-sword.co.uk

Or

PEN AND SWORD BOOKS
1950 Lawrence Rd, Havertown, PA 19083, USA
E-mail: Uspen-and-sword@casematepublishers.com
Website: www.penandswordbooks.com

Contents

Introduction

By 1944 Japan was well and truly on the defensive. In Burma, their offensive towards Imphal and Kohima had failed and by July British and Commonwealth troops were pushing them back into Central Burma. On all fronts the Japanese were being pushed back – serious thought had to be given to future defence.

   The result of these deep deliberations was what would become known as the "Absolute National Defence Sphere", a line drawn in the sand to be held at all costs. Part of the Defence

Pre-war Koror, Palau Islands mandated to the Japanese following the defeat of Germany in WWI (the Palaus were a German protectorate before WWI)

Sphere was the defence of the Palau Islands and, in 1944, after meetings and consultation, Premier Tojo summoned Lt General Inoue, whose 14th Infantry Division had been transferred from mainland China to Saipan but was now to be diverted to the Palau Islands. There General Inoue was to prepare defences and ready himself for the anticipated allied invasion force.

The Palau Islands had first been seized by the Japanese after declaring war on Germany in August of 1914, with Admiral Tatsuo Matsumara landing on Koror in October of that year. Despite American opposition, the League of Nations awarded mandate of the islands to Japan in 1920. During the intervening years between WW1 and the outbreak of WW2, Japan established a major presence on the Palaus, centred on Koror, with a civil government and major Japanese commercial activity. But following the outbreak of hostilities in December 1941 the Palau islands took on a more important role, in the first instance as a forward supply base and training area for the Japanese conquests of 1941 and 1942, but now they were to form part of the front line of the defence of the homeland.

Before the arrival of General Inoue and his forces, the Palau Islands were defended by troops under the command of Major General Yamaguchi, whose troops would now bolster Inoue's forces in defence of the Palaus.

Following detailed surveys, the Japanese assumed correctly that the Allies would probably assault from the south with landings on Peleliu for its airstrip and Angaur, then making their way up the Palau chain heading for Koror and Babelthuap. In reality though this would become unnecessary to the Allies who were able to neutralise the Japanese forces on these islands with their air and naval supremacy.

In the Central Pacific, General Douglas MacArthur's forces had, since 1942, worked their way up from Guadalcanal through the Solomons chain of New Georgia, Bougainville, New

Phosphate loading pier, Angaur.

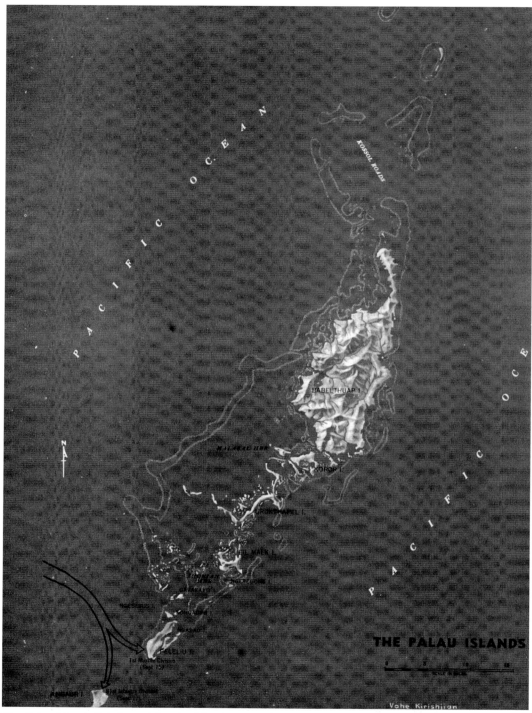

The Palau Islands. Peleliu and Angaur islands are at the southernmost tip of the island group

Britain and Cape Gloucester and across New Guinea. In the early days of 1942 General MacArthur was ordered to leave the Philippines by President Roosevelt, giving his promise to the Philippine people of "I shall return": he was now ready to fulfil that promise. In the Northern Pacific, Admiral Nimitz's forces had a successful "island hopping" campaign from Tarawa in the Gilbert Islands to Guam, Saipan and Tinian in the Marianas, and now had their sights firmly set on Iwo Jima, Okinawa and ultimately the Japanese homeland. Successful carrier-based air strikes on the Japanese naval bases at Truk in the Caroline Islands and Rabaul in the Solomons had neutralised them sufficiently for them to 'wither on the vine' and they were no longer a barrier to progress. MacArthur was determined to return to the Philippines as early as possible and in July of 1944 met with President Roosevelt and Admiral Nimitz in Honolulu, arguing with them that failure to fulfil his pledge to return as soon as possible would have not only an adverse effect on the Philippines, but would also diminish America's prestige amongst friends and allies in the Far East. MacArthur's skill in persuasion was such that he even won over Admiral Nimitz, to the extent of once again securing the loan of the 1st Marine Division as he had previously done for the re-taking of the Solomon Islands. MacArthur always referred to the 1st Marine Division as "My Marines".

Admiral Nimitz had already issued a warning order for invasion of the Palau Islands group, applying the codename of Operation Stalemate.

Chapter One

Opposing Plans, American and Japanese

Initially the plan was for MacArthur to push northwards from New Guinea to Morotai, then on to the Philippines. When the Philippines were safely back in the hands of the US the decision could be taken as to whether an assault could be made on the Japanese mainland via Formosa and China – favoured by MacArthur – or from Okinawa and the Ryukyu Islands – favoured by Nimitz. On September 15 1944, the same day that MacArthur's troops landed on Morotai, the 1st Marine Division, supported by the Army's 81st Wildcat Division, were to make landings on the southern Palau islands of Angaur and Peleliu, part of Operation Stalemate II, this being the revised plan for the assault on the Palau Islands.

As Commander of the Western Pacific Task Force, Admiral Bill Halsey was in overall charge of supporting operations. Whilst the invasion force was ploughing onward towards the Palaus he carried out air strikes from carrier-based planes on the southern and central Philippines and the Palau Islands as part of the pre-invasion preparation.

It soon became apparent from these air strikes that although severe damage to enemy shipping and aircraft was inflicted, raids on the Philippines were lightly contested, suggesting to Halsey that they were not as heavily defended as had at first been believed. Being convinced of this, Halsey ordered his Chief of Staff, Rear Admiral Carney, to send an urgent message to Admiral Nimitz on 13 September, which was only two days ahead of the planned assaults on Morotai and the Palaus, with the following recommendations:

1) Plans for the seizure of Morotai and the Palaus to be abandoned
2) The ground forces which had been identified for these purposes should be diverted to MacArthur for deployment in the Philippines
3) The invasion of Leyte should be carried out as early as possible

Upon receipt of this urgent message, Admiral Nimitz reacted promptly to Halsey's suggestions and sent his own communication to the Joint Chiefs of Staff, at that time in Quebec for the Octagon Conference with President Roosevelt and Prime Minister Churchill. Following consultation by the Chiefs of Staff with General MacArthur, it was decided on September 14, D –1 on Peleliu, that the landings on Leyte would be brought forward by two months, as per the recommendation by Halsey to Nimitz under point 3. The remaining points of Halsey's communique were ignored. Whilst having little effect on the troops who were assaulting Morotai, the same could not be said for the 1st Marine Division and the 81st Infantry Division, the result of this decision costing them more than 9,500 casualties.

Admiral Nimitz never explained his decision to overrule Halsey, merely stating that invasion forces were already at sea and the commitment made, making it too late to call off the invasion. The Palau Islands had very good airfields from which air attacks on an invasion force against the Philippines could be launched. In addition, there were several thousand first rate troops who could be despatched to reinforce the Philippine garrison. Whilst Halsey insisted that both these factors could be dealt with using air strikes and naval bombardments, without committing ground troops, Nimitz still overruled him.

Halsey always disagreed with Nimitz's decisions on Morotai and the Palaus, claiming that the operation of taking the airfields and anchorages afforded by the Palaus, whilst being of great value, would be too costly in terms of manpower. Many of the soldiers and Marines on Peleliu would agree with this view.

On 29 May 1944 Admiral Chester Nimitz, Commander-in-Chief Pacific Fleet and Commander-in-Chief Pacific Ocean Areas (CINCPAC-CINCPOA) issued orders for plans to be drawn up for invasion of the Palau Islands; the operation would have the codename Operation Stalemate. The assault would be carried out in the south by III Amphibious Corps (IIIAC) under the command of Major General Roy S Geiger, USMC, against the islands of Peleliu and Angaur. Running concurrently would be the landing of XXIV Corps on the northern Palau island of Babelthuap. Target date was September 1944. Shortly after operational planning began, numerous problems became evident. The invasion of Guam had fallen behind schedule and was tying up IIIAC and the 77th Infantry Division, both included in Operation Stalemate. In addition, continued requirements in the Marianas meant that much of the shipping for Stalemate was also unavailable. Intelligence was gathered using aerial and reconnaissance photographs and in June 1944 the submarine USS Seawolf carried out photographic reconnaissance of the invasion landing beaches. Further reconnaissance was carried out on Peleliu and Yap beaches by submarine USS Burrfish, from which an eleven man reconnaissance team landed on the Peleliu beaches for a closer investigation in respect of water depth, location of potholes and sand bars. This was similarly checked on the Yap beaches, however only two of the five man reconnaissance team returned to the pick up point. Despite several attempts to locate those missing, they were unsuccessful and the remaining two returned to the Burrfish. Following this incident, Admiral Nimitz banned any further missions of this type.

The investigations however revealed a large Japanese garrison on Babelthuap, also that the island was only suitable for limited facilities, including airstrip. There was therefore no justifiable tactical reason to invade Babelthuap which resulted in CINCPOA issuing a second warning order to cancel the operation and replace it with a revision of the original plan, codename Operation Stalemate II.

In terms of significant intelligence information, some of the most useful to come the Americans' way was from the island of Saipan following its fall in July 1944. Files were captured of the Japanese 31st Army Headquarters and these, added to the capture by chance of a Japanese intelligence officer, revealed the organisation table for both Peleliu and Angaur garrisons. The tables identified troop strengths on Peleliu at 10,500 and on Angaur at approximately 1,400 men.

The revised Operation Stalemate II plan included, as in the original, the assault on the islands of Peleliu and Angaur by IIIAC. However, one change to the original plan was the floating reserve of the 77th Infantry Division, with the 5th Marine Division in general reserve, the latter being at that time based on Hawaii. D-Day would be 15 September 1944, with the second phase on October 8 1944 requiring XXIV Corps to assault the islands of Yap and Ulithi, thereby substituting the 96th Infantry Division of the 77th Infantry who were now in reserve for IIIAC.

The planners considered four combinations of beaches for the assault on Peleliu as follows:

1) Purple Beach to the south had the advantage of a narrow reef which in one area facilitated the possibility of bringing conventional landing craft all the way up to the beach. Unfortunately the Japanese had already identified this as being suitable for landings and had allocated their strongest defences. Another factor was the dense mangrove swamp just inland from the beach which narrowed the area considerably and had made it perfect for defence. Purple Beach was therefore rejected.
2) Scarlet Beach on the south west, in conjunction with Orange beaches, was discarded due to the danger of assault troops possibly converging and being caught up in friendly fire.
3) Amber Beach on the north west — here the reef was at its widest and the northern flank was under enfilading fire from nearby Ngesebus Island. Around 300 yards inland the low beach gave way to dominating higher ground, failure to take which could expose the beachhead to murderous artillery fire. For these reasons, Amber Beach was also rejected.
4) There remained White and Orange Beaches to the west which, as they favoured a direct drive across the island from west to east, were the option considered to be the most viable and subsequently the chosen option.

The initial assault would combine three Regimental Combat Teams (RCTs) to land abreast, namely the 1st, 5th and 7th Marines. Each would have one of their 3 Battalions as Regimental and Divisional reserve. The 1st Marines, less the Battalion in regimental reserve, were to land on the left flank on White Beaches 1 and 2, pushing inland to a pre-determined point. They would then wheel left and attack the nose of the ridge which extended up the north western peninsula. The 1st Marines would then advance along this peninsula, the coastal plain and the high ground, all the way to the northern tip of Peleliu, then on to Ngesebus island, supported by the 5th Marines on the right flank. In the central area, the 5th Marines were to land one Battalion on each of Orange Beaches 1 and 2. The left would tie up with the 1st Marines with the remainder driving across straight to the eastern shore. The 3rd Battalion were to land at H+1 hour and would move between the other two Battalions, participating the move northwards. The 7th Marines on the right flank were to land two Battalions in column on Orange Beach 3, keeping their 3rd Battalion as Divisional reserve. The two Battalions ashore would drive across to the eastern shore flanking the 5th Marines. They would then wheel right and clean up the isolated enemy forces whilst driving on to the southern tip of the island.

When the assault on Peleliu was considered to be "well in hand", and only at this time, the 81st Infantry Division was detailed to assault the island of Angaur but until then they were to remain Corps Reserve. The assault on Angaur would be undertaken by two of the 81st Infantry's three Regimental Combat Teams whilst the third would be sent north to Ulithi. The date for this assault on Angaur would be determined by the 1st Marine Division Commander. Landings would take place on two beaches simultaneously, the 322nd RCT landing on northern Red Beach. They would then push inland, south and west across the island, the left flank tying in with the second assault team, the 321st RCT. The 321st would have landed on Blue Beach in the west and would move inland west and south across the island, the right flank tying in with the 332nd RCT left. After securing Angaur, the 81st Infantry would initially revert to Corps reserve, later to garrison Peleliu and Angaur once they were declared secure. The 1st Marine Division were to return to their base on Pavuvu Island.

The Americans anticipated that these operations on Peleliu and Angaur would be completed within one week: General Rupertus stating "It will be a short operation, a hard-fought "quickie" that will last 3 days and may only take 2 and may result in a considerable number of casualties. You can be sure, however, that the 1st Division will conquer Peleliu". Rupertus was proved right about the "Considerable casualties", but the 1st Marine Division alone would not take Peleliu and it would take months, not days, before Peleliu was taken.

From the Japanese perspective, considering the loss of the Marshall Islands and heavy raids on Truk and the Carolina Islands, they needed a serious re-think in relation to defending the homelands from the pending invasion by the Allies. Initially the defence of the Palau Islands, which consisted mainly of air and sea transport units, defence battalions and rear echelon units, was entrusted to Major General Yamaguchi. However, following the collapse of the Japanese outer frontier the various island garrisons took on greater significance as a part of the new "Absolute National Defense Sphere".

The fall of the Marshall islands and neutralisation of Truk, combined with carrier-based air strikes on the Caroline islands, increased significantly the possibility of a US invasion of the Palau islands. With this in mind, the 14th Infantry Division, which had been transferred from mainland China to New Guinea and re-directed to Saipan, was now diverted to the Palaus, arriving in April 1944. The Commander of the 14th Division, Lt General Inoue, established headquarters on Koror island, retaining most of his troops on Koror and Babelthuap, both of which he considered would be likely targets for the Americans' invasion. The 2nd Regiment (Reinforced), 14th Division, which was under the command of Colonel Nakagawa, was sent south to garrison and construct defences on the islands of Peleliu and Angaur.

In order to effect the defence of Peleliu, Colonel Nakagawa split the island into four defence districts, namely north, south, east and west. North District would be defended by the 346th Independent Infantry Battalion, commanded by Major Hikino, South District defended by the 3rd Battalion, 15th Infantry Regiment under the command of Captain Chiaki, East District defended by the 3rd Battalion, 2nd Infantry Regiment under the command of Captain Harada and West District defended by the 2nd Battalion, 2nd Infantry Regiment commanded by Major Timita. Additionally, support units of artillery, tanks and engineers would be in place. Japanese plans were set for defence of the beaches in addition to a defence in depth, which followed closely those set out by Koror headquarters in the "Palau Group Sector Training for Victory" order, issued on 11 July 1944. In this document, Headquarters stated that "the ultimate goal of this training is to minimize our losses in the severe enemy pre-landing naval and aerial bombardment and, on the very night of the enemy landing, to take advantage of the fact that their equipment is not fully consolidated, to destroy their bridgehead at one blow...".

Even though Peleliu would eventually be taken by the Americans, the concept of setting out well thought out defences both on the beaches and in depth would prove to have been a sound notion. It was considered that small-scale coordinated counter attacks over a more protracted period rather than the previous frenzied 'Banzai' charges, which had resulted in a needless waste of life, would prove more effective in "bleeding the Americans white", in addition to providing an opportunity to buy sufficient time for Japan to negotiate peace. Unfortunately for the Japanese, this opportunity did not arise.

The plan also stated that "we must recognise the limits of naval and aerial bombardment. Every soldier and civilian employee will remain unmoved by this, must strengthen his spirits even while advancing by utilising lulls in enemy bombardment and taking advantage of the terrain according to necessity…". Nakagawa did this to great effect, taking full advantage of the numerous caves and sink holes, particularly in the Umurbrogol Ridges area. There would be no mass suicidal banzai charges; rather a prolonged war of attrition designed to bleed the Americans white. This new tactic would be new to the Americans at Peleliu, however it would subsequently be experienced in other encounters, in particular Iwo Jima and Okinawa.

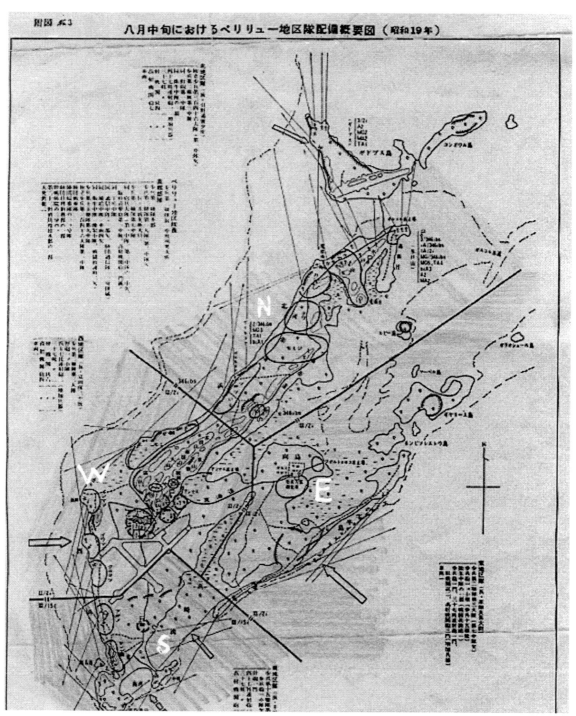

Japanese defence map of Peleliu. Lt Col Nakagawa divided Peleliu into four defence quadrants – N, S, E and W

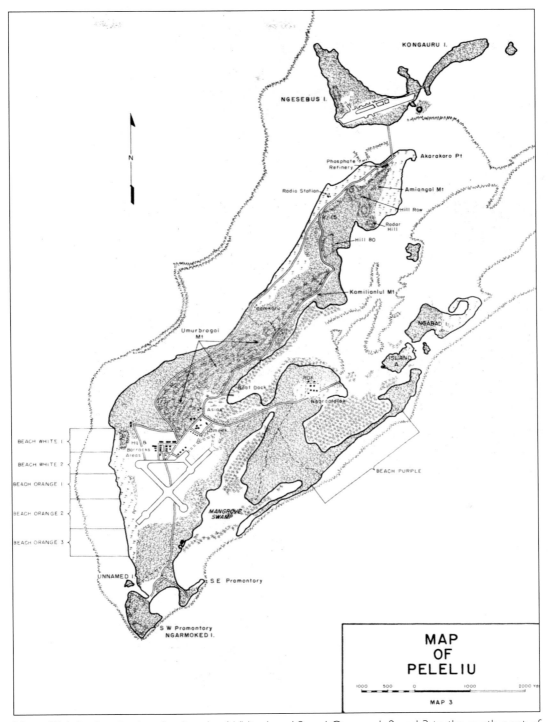

Map of Peleliu showing invasion beaches White 1 and 2 and Orange, 1, 2 and 3 to the south-west of the island.

Beach Scarlet, Peleliu. Photograph taken after the island had been secured. Rejected as one of the landing beaches due to the danger of converging on troops advancing inland from Orange Beaches

Chapter Two

Opposing Forces and Commanders

The Americans assembled an impressive force as part of the Third Fleet expeditionary troops for the invasion of Peleliu. Labelled "Stalemate II", this force was commanded by Major General Julian C Smith, direct command of the Western Task Force (Southern Palaus) being by III Amphibious Corps under the command of Major General Roy S Geiger. The main assault troops for III Amphibious Corps were the 1st Marine Division (Reinforced) and the US Army 81st Infantry "Wildcat" Division.

Battleships Pennsylvania, Maryland, Mississippi, Tennessee and Idaho, with heavy cruisers Columbus, Indianapolis, Louisville, Minneapolis and Portland and light cruisers Cleveland, Denver and Honolulu would provide pre-invasion bombardment, supported by planes from 3 large carriers and 5 light carriers. This pre-invasion preparation on Peleliu would commence on D-3, which was 12 September 1944, and would continue until and including D-Day, 15 September 1944. However, on D-1 – 14 September 1944 – Admiral Oldenorf reported that he had run out of targets and was aborting the bombardment. The majority of the naval support vessels were sent to the Philippines in support of the upcoming landings.

Operation Stalemate II consisted of two attack plans for the assault of the Palau Islands, the first being the island of Peleliu, which would be assaulted by the 1st Marine Division (Reinforced), designation TG32.1. The second phase was to be the assault of Angaur Island, on the south west side of Peleliu, this phase being the target for the Army's 81st Division, designation TG32.2. The 1st Marine Division (Reinforced) was to comprise three Infantry Regiments in addition to Divisional and Support Battalions of motor transport, pioneer, engineer and medical. These three Infantry Regiments consisted of the 1st Marines under the command of Col Lewis B (Chesty) Puller, the 5th Marines under the command of Col Harold D (Bucky) Harris and the 7th Marines under the command of Col Herman H (Hard-headed) Hanneken. Marine Regiments are always designated as Marines, therefore 1st Marine Regiment is referred to as "1st Marines" and so on. These were RCT (Regimental Combat Teams) 1, 5 and 7 with the codenames of Spitfire, Lone Wolf and Mustang respectively. Corps reserve was the Army 81st Infantry Division – "Wildcat" Division – minus the 323rd RCT which, under the command of Col Arthur P Watson, would be assaulting Ulithi Atoll which is located between the Palaus to the south and the Marianas to the north east. The other two RCTs would assault the island of Angaur after release by the 1st Marine Division commander,

Major General Rupertus, as and when he was of the opinion that the situation on Peleliu did not require assistance from the 81st Infantry.

The 81st Infantry Division would use two of its three RCTs– namely the 321st and 322nd – with supporting units for the assault on Angaur, these RCTs being under the command of Col Robert Dark and Col Benjamin Venable respectively. In overall command of the 81st Infantry was Major General Paul Mueller (USA).

In total, the number of assault troops for Stalemate II was approximately 2647 officers and 44914 enlisted men, of which 1438 officers and 24979 enlisted men were Marines. The breakdown of this total was to be:

Expeditionary troops under Commanding General Major General Julian C Smith and Chief of Staff Dudley S Brown

The 7th Anti-aircraft artillery battalion under Lt Colonel Henry R Paige, which landed on Angaur on 21 September and remained as part of the garrison force)

Corps Troops as below:
1st Amphibious Tractor Battalion under Major Albert Reutlinger (until 21 September) and Capt Arthur J Noonan (from 22 September)
6th Amphibious Tractor Battalion – Capt John I Fitzgerald Jr
8th Amphibious Tractor Battalion – Lt Col Charles B Nerren
3rd Armored Amphibious Battalion – Lt Col Kimber H Boyer
12th Anti-aircraft Artillery Battalion – lt col Merlyn D Holmes
3rd 155mm Howitzer Battalion – Lt Col Richard A Evans
8th 155mm Gun Battalion – Maj George V Hanna Jr
1st Tank Battalion – Lt Col Arthur J (Jeb) Stuart
1st Service Battalion – Col John Kaluf
Divisional Headquarters – Col Joseph F Hankins (who was killed in action on 3 October) and Lt Col Austin C Shofner (from 3 October)
1st Motor Transport Battalion – Capt Tobert B McBroom
1st Pioneer Battalion – Lt Col Robert G Balance
1st Engineer Battalion – Lt Col Levi W Smith Jr
1st Medical Battalion – Commander (MC) Emil E Napp

Before they were relieved by the 81st Infantry Division, almost all the 1st Division service troops would be committed as infantry.

The 1st Marine Division (Reinforced) – Major General H Rupertus was made up as follows:

1st Marine Regiment (1st Marines) – Col Lewis B Puller
5th Marine Regiment (5th Marines) – Col Harold D Harris
7th Marine Regiment (7th Marines) – Col Herman H Hanneken
11th Marine Regiment (11th Marines – Artillery) – Col William H Harrison

The 81st Infantry Division (US Army) – Major General Paul J Mueller was made up as follows:

a. RCT 321:   Colonel Robert F Dark, Commanding
   321 Inf
   316 FA Bn
   Co A 306 Engr Bn plus Det H&S Co
   Co A plus Co D (less 2d Plat) and Hq 306 Med Bn (less Det)
   Det 781 Ord (LM) Co
   Det Traf Sqd 81 MP Plat
   Det 81 QM Co
   154 Engr (C) Bn plus Det Hq & Hq Co 1138 Engr (C) Gp
   Det 592 JAS Co
   Det 481 Amph Truck Co
   Co A 726 Amph Tractor Bn plus Det H&S Co ½ Co D 776 Amph Tank Bn
   Co A 710 Tank Bn
   Det Prov QM Gr Reg Co
   Det Translator-Intpr Team "A" Hq Co CPA
b. RCT 322:   Colonel B W Venable, Commanding
   322 Inf
   317 FA Bn
   Co B 306 Engr Bn plus Det H&S Co
   Co B 306 Med Bn
   Det 781 Ord (LM) Co
   Det Traf Sqd 81 MP Plat
   52 Engr (C) Bn plus Det Hq & Hq Co 1138 Engr (C) Gp
   Det 592 JAS Co
   Co B 710 Tank Bn
   Co D 88 Cml Wpns Bn
   726 Amph Tractor Bn (less Co A & Det H&S Co)
   Co D 776 Amph Tank Bn (less ½ Co)
   Det Translator-Intpr Team "A" Hq Co CPA
   17 Field Hosp (less 1 Plat)
   Det Prov QM Gr Reg Co
c. RCT 323:   Colonel A P Watson, Commanding
   323 Inf
   906 FA Bn
   Co C 306 Engr Bn plus Det H&S Co
   Co C plus 2d Plat Co D and Det Hq 306 Med Bn
   Det 781 Ord (LM) Co
   Det Traf Sqd 81 MP Plat
   Det 81 QM Co
   Det 481 Amph Tractor Co
   Det 592 JAS Co
   155 Engr (C) Bn plus Det Hq & Hq Co 1138 Engr (C) Gp
   Det Prov QM Gr Reg Co
   Det Translator-Intpr Team "A" Hq Co CPA

2. Division Troops (less CTS) are as follows:
    81 Div Hq
    Hq Sp Trs 81 Div
        Hq Co 81 Div
            81st CIC Det
            1 Photo Asgmt Unit 3116 Sig Sv Bn
            Translator-Intpr Team "A" Hq Co
                CPA (less 3 dets)
        81 MP Plat (less 3 dets)
        81 Div Band
        781 Ord (LM) Co (less 3 dets)
            104 Bomb Disposal Sqd (Garrison Forces ANGAUR)
        81 QM Co (less 2 dets)
            2d Plat 3259 QM Serv Co (Garrison Force ANGAUR)
            3rd Plat 247 QM Depot Co (Garrison Force ANGAUR)
        81 Sig Co
        481 Amph Truck Co (less 3 Dets)
        592 JAS Co (less 3 Dets)
        405 Ord Med Maint Co (Garrison Force ANGAUR)
        1st Plat Prov QM Gr Reg Co (less 3 Dets)
    81 Div Arty (less 3 light Bns)
    81 Cav Rcn Tr
    306 Engr Bn (less 3 Cos and Detes H&S Co)
    306 Med Bn (less 4 Cos and Hq Dets)
    41st Portable Surg Hosp
    1 Plat 17th Field Hosp
    Hq & Hq Co 1138 Engr (C) Gp (less Dets)
        290 Port Co (Garrison Force ANGAUR)
        3d Depot Plat 722 Engr Depot Co (Garrison Force ANGAUR)
    710 Tank Bn (less 2 Cos)
    483 AAA (AW) Bn
    7 AAA Bn (Marine) (-) (Garrison Force ANGAUR)

By command of MAJOR GENERAL PAUL J MUELLER:

The Naval Commanders of the Third Amphibious Force, despite being in overall command of Stalemate II, had little or no input into the planning of the invasion of the Palau islands and ceased to be in control of the situation after the ground troops landed. In August 1943, Vice Admiral Theodore S Wilkinson had succeeded Admiral Richard Kelly Turner as the Commander of the Third Amphibious Force. He was an advocate of the "hit them where they ain't" philosophy and was considered to be an intellectual. His flag officers – namely Admirals Fort, Oldendorf, Blandy, Ainsworth, Kingman and Ofstie – had all previously had combat experience in liaison with Marine and Army units. Despite evidence of previous difficulties between the Navy and Marine/Army units, there is no evidence to suggest that the units engaged in Stalemate II experienced any such discord.

General Julian C Smith, previously commander of the 2nd Marine Division on Tarawa, was in command of the Expeditionary Troops Third Fleet. Julian Smith was recognised as an expert in amphibious warfare and found this new position difficult, being of the opinion that he held little authority under the watchful eyes of Navy and Marine senior officers, and considered his role to be that of overseeing administrative, logistical and tactical units. He said of his role "I filed papers". He was placed in temporary command of III Amphibious Corps as cover for General Roy S Geiger, appointed Commander, who was still engaged in operations on Guam in the Marianas.

In addition to the temporary role of being in charge of planning for Stalemate II, Julian Smith still had to carry out his duties as Commander, Expeditionary Troops, Third Fleet, allowing less time than he would have preferred to check the finer details. One of these details was that General Rupertus, Commanding General of the 1st Marine Division, had suffered a broken ankle during landing practice. With a little more notice whilst planning for the upcoming assault, Smith would have relieved Rupertus of command of the 1st Division, but the information was gleaned too late for this to be implemented.

Eventually Major General Roy S Geiger, at almost 60 years old, was in overall command of III Amphibious Corps. Geiger had commanded aviation units in both world wars and his career had been mostly in aviation, including the 1st Marine Air Wing on Guadalcanal. Geiger was appointed Director of Marine Corps Aviation in 1943 and then returned to the Pacific as Commander of I Marine Amphibious Corps. He would not assume command of III Amphibious Corps and Operation Stalemate II until 15 August 1944, due to his involvement in the protracted assault on the Marianas, and therefore far too late to be able to influence the planning.

Major General William H Rupertus was in overall command of the 1st Marine Division – the assaulting troops on Peleliu. Rupertus was 55 years of age and a good friend of fellow Marine Generals Holland and Julian Smith and Vandegrift who was commanding officer of the 1st Marine Division. Upon Vandegrift's promotion to Commandant of the Marine Corps, Rupertus was the obvious choice of successor to the role of commanding General of the 1st Marine Division. Rupertus, in common with his fellow 1st Division officers, had seen overseas duty before WW2 including commanding the 1st Battalion, 4th Marines in Shanghai in 1937 when the Japanese had occupied the city. During this particular tour of duty Rupertus tragically lost his wife, daughter and son to a Typhoid epidemic, which affected him deeply, causing him to become moody and suffer bouts of depression. This had a serious effect on his relationships with subordinates and would become more apparent in the battle of Peleliu.

Rupertus also had an obvious mistrust of the Army, a feeling shared with many in the Marine Corps, mainly due to basic differences of opinion regarding the conduct of battles. As such, Rupertus considered it unnecessary for the Army's 81st Division to be reserve for his 1st Marine Division and made it clear that he had no intention whatsoever to ask for their assistance.

The team of commanders from the US Marine Corps for this battle consisted of highly distinguished leaders; the three assault regiments of the 1st Marine Division being the 1st, 5th and 7th Marines. In command of the 1st Marines, who were to land on the left flank, was Colonel Lewis B (Chesty) Puller, probably the most well-known of the three Regimental Commanders. Colonel Puller was a Virginian, having entered the Corps as a teenager and served with distinction in the majority of the Marine Corps "Banana Wars" prior to WW2 in the Caribbean, Haiti and Nicaragua. Also prior to the war he had served in China and commanded the Horse Marine detachment in Shanghai in 1933. It was during this time that he became known as a 'no-nonsense' commander with a strong dislike of the Japanese. Chesty Puller considered that a commander led from the front and by 1944 had become legendary as a result. On Guadalcanal, command of the 1st Battalion, 7th Marines, as Lieutenant Colonel led to him receiving his third Navy Cross. Strong leadership skills coupled with versatility in a variety of roles on New Britain resulted in promotion to command of the 1st Marines in February 1944.

On the right flank landing would be by the 7th Marines who were commanded by Colonel Herman ("Hard headed") Hanneken. Hanneken, like Puller, was involved in the pre-WW2 campaigns in Haiti and Nicaragua and, in 1919, as an enlisted Marine and holding the rank of Captain in the Haitan Gendarmerie, he had, with one other Marine, infiltrated the rebel Caco headquarters and killed their leader, Charlemagne Peratte. For this action he was awarded the Congressional Medal of Honor and would repeat this exercise almost identically ten years later on Nicaragua, capturing Manuel Jiron, who was one of Cesar Sandino's leading lieutenants. Hanneken went on to command a battalion on Guadalcanal and was Chief of Staff to the Assistant Divisional Commander before taking command of the 7th Marines in February 1944. He was the oldest of the three Regimental Commanders and was a Marine of the "Old Corps". He was never known to smile, but had an intense dedication to duty; his loyalty and personal courage earning him the utmost respect from both his men and his fellow officers, as well as a reputation as a tough, brave and fearless commander.

Landings in the centre would be undertaken by the 5th Marines commanded by Colonel Harold D (Bucky) Harris who was the youngest of the three Regimental Commanders. Unlike Puller and Hanneken, Harris was a career officer and had not been an enlisted Marine. He was commissioned following graduation from Annapolis in 1925 and attended Army Infantry School at Fort Benning, where he graduated in 1935. He was then one of the few Americans to attend the Ecole Superieure de Guerre in Paris in 1938/39. He went on to serve in various posts in the USA at Philadelphia, Quantico, San Diego and Parris Island and overseas in China and Nicaragua. He was stationed in Marine Intelligence Section, Washington DC at the outbreak of WW2 and in July 1942 transferred in the post of Intelligence Officer to the staff of Commander, Amphibious Forces, South Pacific. He was for a brief time Chief of Staff, Marine Forces Solomons, in 1943 before being assigned to the 1st Marine Division in the post of Executive Officer, 1st Marines, where he served through the New Britain campaign before his appointment as Divisional Assistant Chief of Staff, Intelligence, in February 1944. He was given command of the 5th Marines prior to the invasion of Peleliu and, although he was new to the 5th Marines and to combat, they would go on to perform well on Peleliu under his command.

The 81st Infantry Division, commanded by Major General Paul J Meuller USA was the reserve for the III Amphibious Corps. General Meuller was a competent commander, having led his division through several months' training on mainland USA and the Jungle Warfare Centre on Hawaii. Although they were lacking combat experience, Mueller believed that his 81st 'Wildcats' were as ready for the forthcoming assault on Peleliu at the 1st Marine Division.

Japanese Command – Palau

The Palau group came under the command of Lieutenant General Sadai Inoue, with the 14th Infantry Division of Kwangtung fame. The garrison of Army and Navy personnel in the Palau Islands had been greatly increased and Lt Gen Inoue was Tojo's choice of commander. Inoue was of medium build, a strict disciplinarian with a stern voice, and came from a heritage of five generations of military officers. He was considered by General Tojo to be absolutely competent and well suited to take command of the Palaus garrison with its mixture of troops. His lack of flair was balanced by his utmost tenacity and he was unlikely to collapse under adversity.

Following aerial reconnaissance General Inoue concluded that Peleliu, Ngesebus and Angaur, to the south of the Palaus chain, would be the major islands in his line of defence. Peleliu had been garrisoned prior to the arrival of Inoue by the Navy, with 7,000 Naval Defense Troops and some Korean labour troops, under the command of Vice Admiral Seiichi Itou. Under his command, by 1944 blockhouses, bunkers and reinforced concrete defences had been constructed, adding to the natural defences already in situ such as caves and tunnels, which had been expanded and improved by Itou's men.

General Inoue, however, had headquarters on Koror Island, which is north of Peleliu, from where he deployed around 35,000 troops in the Palaus, consisting of the 14th Division, 53rd Independent Mixed Brigade and units of the 1st Amphibious Brigade. He also sent a further 8-10,000 troops to garrison Yap Island. Since he considered that Babelthuap would be the most likely island for the American invasion he stationed around 25,000 troops there and sent the 2nd Infantry Regiment (reinforced) under the command of Colonel Kunio Nakagawa to take over from the Navy the defence of Peleliu. Colonel Nakagawa commanded the joint Army and Navy defence force numbering 10,500 troops on Peleliu plus 1,400 troops on Angaur.

The Palaus were – and had long been – considered to be a Japanese naval command area. An inter-service rivalry occurred between the Army and the Navy in April 1944, when the Army arrived to take command of all ground forces. In order to resolve this problem and its threat to preparations for the defence of Peleliu, Lt Gen Inoue dispatched Maj Gen Kenjiro Murai in an effort to supply the Army with sufficient rank to the local naval commander whilst at the same time putting operational mission control firmly with Nakagawa.

Colonel Nakagawa's Army Defence Force for Peleliu and Angaur was:

2nd Infantry regiment	Colonel Nakagawa (IJA)
	Executive officer Captain Sakamoto
346th Independent Infantry Battalion	Major Hikino
3rd Battalion, 15th Infantry Regiment	Captain Chiaki
3rd Battalion, 2nd Infantry Regiment	Captain Harada
2nd Battalion, 2nd Infantry Regiment	Major Tomota
1st Battalion, 818th Field Artillery Regiment	Major Kobayashi
14th Division tank Company (approx. 12-15 tanks)	Captain Amano
Engineer Company	1st Lt Isohata

In addition to Vice Admiral Itou's Naval Defence force and Korean labour troops, this made a total of approximately 10 – 11,000 officers and enlisted men of which approximately 6.300 were combat troops, the remainder being labour troops or airbase personnel. Weaponry at Nakagawa's disposal consisted of 24 75mm cannons, 13-15 light tanks, 15 81mm mortars, 4 150mm mortars, 30 dual-purpose AA guns, nearly 100 .50-cal machine guns, dozens of light machine guns and a number of naval anti-aircraft guns and rudimentary rocket launchers for sending up large, unguided naval shells.

For Operation Stalemate II, the objective of the US Army's 81st Division was the island of Angaur, which was defended by 1st Battalion 59th Infantry (IJA) commanded by Major Ushio Goto and comprising approximately 1,400 officers and enlisted men. American intelligence, however, had estimated that the Japanese forces on Angaur were in the region of 2,500 combat troops.

USS *Gillespie* (DD 609) pulls away after transferring mail to USS *DuPage* (APA 41) while en-route to Peleliu, 13 September 1944. (*National Museum of the US Navy*)

Navajo Indians from Arizona played an important part in maintaining communication at Peleliu. They are, front row, left to right: Pfc Billy Cleveland of Red Lake, Fort Defiance; Pfc Nelson A Brown of Thunderbird Ranch, Chinle; Pfc Alfred Tah of Chinle; Pfc San Tsosie of Star Route, Winslow; Pfc Alex Williams of Leupp. Rear row, left to right: Pfc Dennis Cattlechaser of Tuba City; Pfc Thomas Claw of Chinle; Pfc Joe H. Kellwood of Steamboat Canyon, Ganado; Pfc Carl Crawford of Ganado; Pfc Wallace Peshlakai of Twin Peaks; Pfc Layton Paddock of Winslow. In the foreground, commending them for their work is Marine Lieutenant Colonel James C. Smith, First Marine Division signal officer. (*NARA*)

Vice Admiral Seiichi Itou (IJN). Originally in command of the defences of the Palau islands, Itou was replaced by Lt General Sadao Inoue (IJA), commander of the Japanese 14th Army Division, transferred from Manchuria to the Palaus

Major General Kenjiro Murai, sent from Koro by General Inoue to support Col Nakagawa, who was having great difficulty getting cooperation from the IJN command on Peleliu. Murai outranked both Commanders but was happy to let Nakagawa get on with the job of defending Peleliu. Murai's and Nakagawa's remains were recovered in 1993

Lt Col Kunio Nakagawa (IJA), Commander of the 2nd Infantry Regiment (reinforced) sent to Peleliu to command the defences of Peleliu and Angaur

Admiral Chester Nimitz, Commander-in-Chief, Pacific Fleet and Commander-in-Chief Pacific Ocean Areas (CINCPAC) was in overall command of Operation Stalemate II: it was his final decision to go ahead with the invasion of Peleliu and Angaur.

Brigadier General Oliver P Smith USMC, second in command of the 1st Marine Division, was left to formulate the assault on Peleliu by General Rupertus. Smith was often kept in the dark by Rupertus

In July 1944 the two Commanders of the Pacific campaign, General Douglas McArthur and Admiral Nimitz, met with President Roosevelt in Hawaii. It was agreed that to protect McArthur's right flank in the forthcoming invasion of the Philippines, the Palau Islands of Peleliu and Angaur would need to be in Allied hands. The job of taking these islands went to Admiral Nimitz; target date was to be 8 September 1944. This date was later changed to 15 September 1944, Operation Stalemate II

Aerial view of the southern end of Peleliu. The invasion beaches and airfield can be clearly seen. The reconnaissance photo taken prior to the invasion.

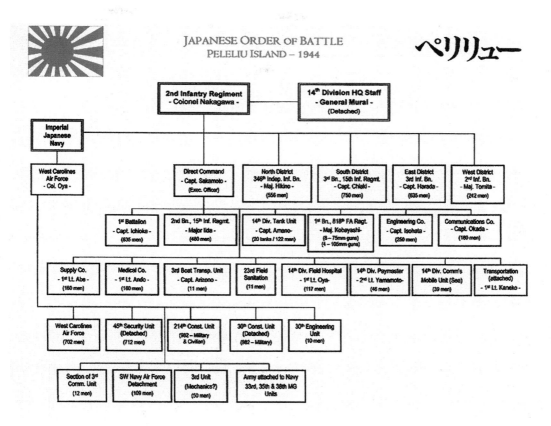

JAPANESE ORDER OF BATTLE
PELELIU ISLAND – 1944

ペリリュー

2nd Infantry Regiment - Colonel Nakagawa -

14th Division HQ Staff - General Murai - (Detached)

Imperial Japanese Navy

West Carolines Air Force - Col. Oya -

Direct Command - Capt. Sakamoto - (Exec. Officer)

North District 346th Indep. Inf. Bn. - Maj. Hikino - (556 men)

South District 3rd Bn., 15th Inf. Regmt. - Capt. Chiaki - (835 men)

East District 3rd Inf. Bn. - Capt. Harada - (835 men)

West District 2nd Inf. Bn. - Maj. Tomita - (242 men)

1st Battalion - Capt. Ichioka - (835 men)

2nd Bn., 15th Inf. Regmt. - Major Iida - (480 men)

14th Div. Tank Unit - Capt. Amano - (20 tanks / 122 men)

1st Bn., 818th FA Regt. - Maj. Kobayashi - (8 – 75mm guns) (4 – 105mm guns)

Engineering Co. - Capt. Isohata - (250 men)

Communications Co. - Capt. Okada - (180 men)

Supply Co. - 1st Lt. Abe - (160 men)

Medical Co. - 1st Lt. Ando - (160 men)

3rd Boat Transp. Unit - Capt. Arizono - (11 men)

23rd Field Sanitation (11 men)

14th Div. Field Hospital - 1st Lt. Oya - (117 men)

14th Div. Paymaster - 2nd Lt. Yamamoto - (46 men)

14th Div. Comm's Mobile Unit (Sea) (39 men)

Transportation (attached) - 1st Lt. Kaneko -

West Carolines Air Force (702 men)

45th Security Unit (Detached) (712 men)

214th Const. Unit (982 – Military & Civilian)

30th Const. Unit (Detached) (982 – Military)

30th Engineering Unit (10 men)

Section of 3rd Comm. Unit (12 men)

SW Navy Air Force Detachment (109 men)

3rd Unit (Mechanics?) (50 men)

Army attached to Navy 33rd, 35th & 38th MG Units

Japanese Order of Battle 1944 Peleliu

Pavuvu, Russel Islands. When the 1st Marine Division was pulled out of the fighting on Cape Gloucester many veterans of Guadalcanal expected to return to Australia for R and R. Instead they were dropped off on the island of Pavuvu, infested with rats, crabs and rotting coconut trees. This did nothing to help the worn out Marines to recover ready for the assault on Peleliu.

Pavuvu; 1st Marine Division load LSTs and LCTs ready for the assault on Peleliu. Note the Marine ambulance Jeep reversing onto the LST, many of the ambulance Jeeps would be needed on Peleliu. In the background is the camouflaged ship Mount McKinley, command ship of Admiral Fort, Commander of the US Navy invasion fleet

Col Lewis B "Chesty" Puller, Commander of the 1st Marines on Peleliu. Puller had served in the Caribbbean 'Banana Wars' and China before the war. Whilst stationed in Shanghai in 1933 Puller acquired a great dislike for the Japanese. He commanded a battalion of the 7th Marines on Guadalcanal, earning him his 3rd Navy Cross (Puller would become the most decorated Marine in Marine Corps history). In February 1944 Puller was promoted to Colonel and given command of the 1st Marines.

Col Herman H "Hard-headed" Hanneken, Commander of the 7th Marines. Like Chesty Puller, Hanneken had served in Haiti and Nicaragua before the war. He had served as an enlisted Marine during WW1. In October 1919 as a Captain in the Haitan Gendarmerie he was awarded the Medal of Honor for almost single-handedly killing a Cacos guerrilla leader. After serving as Chief of Staff and Assistant Divisional Commander, 1st Marine Division, Hanneken was given the command of the 7th Marines for the Peleliu operation in February 1944.

Pavuvu – when the 1st Marine Division was pulled out of the fighting on Cape Gloucester they expected to return to Australia to recover and re-fit as they had done after Guadalcanal. Instead they were deposited on Pavuvu in the Russel Islands, North of Guadalcanal. Nothing was ready for their arrival and it would take months to make the island into somewhere the 1st Marine Division could prepare for their next battle – Peleliu

Maj Gen Roy S Geiger, USMC Commander of
III Amphibious Corps for the Peleliu operation.

Maj Gen William H Rupertus, USMC,
Commanding General 1st Marine Division
(Reinforced) for the Peleliu operation. Not a
flamboyant officer but well thought of by many
high ranking officers, including the Marine Corps
Commandant General A A Vandergrift, former
Commander of the 1st Marine Division. Rupertus
had served overseas before the war, including
China where he clashed several times with
Japanese troops. Also in China Rupertus lost his
wife, daughter and son to illness which left him
with bouts of depression

Pavuvu, men of the 1st Marine Division get acquainted with a new kind of amphibious landing craft, the DUKW amphibious truck, given to the Marines by the Army to bolster the number of Amtracs. The DUKWs had no armour and many were destroyed on D-Day before they could reach shore.

Maj Gen Julian C Smith, USMC,
designated Commander
US Expeditionary Troops –
Operation Stalemate II

Aerial view of the South of Peleliu. At top centre is the all-important airfield, at bottom left the wetlands that divided Peleliu's "Claws" East and West. At right is the Umurbrogol Mountains with the East and West roads that ran the full length of the mountains

Chapter Three

Peleliu D-Day, September 15 1944

September 15 1944 was D-Day on Peleliu. After practice landings on Guadalcanal, men of the 1st Marine Division and the Army's 81st Infantry Division made an uneventful 2100 mile voyage and made preparations for the battle. On board their troop transports, the men checked their weapons and equipment in the pre-dawn light. The men had their traditional steak and eggs breakfast, a ritual adopted by the Marines during their stay in Australia after Guadalcanal and often regretted as they headed towards a beach in a flat-bottomed Amtrac or Higgins boat! Ship's surgeons operating on the wounded would share the same sentiment.

The practice landings had highlighted several mistakes, such as troops being hurriedly loaded onto the wrong transports and then having to be swapped over whilst at sea. The major failing however was that the area identified for practice landings did not have a fringing reef and did not allow rehearsal of transferring from landing craft to Amtrac under rough sea conditions at a reef edge. Hence the practice landings resulted in several casualties suffering broken bones, including General Rupertus, Commanding Officer of the 1st Marine Division, who suffered a broken ankle. Had General Geiger been aware of Rupertus' injury he would have removed him from command of the operation.

Three days before D-Day, on September 12, submerged obstructions had been cleared by underwater demolition teams, who also blasted pathways through the reef to assist the assault troops. This work was highly dangerous, often being carried out whilst under small arms fire from the Japanese defenders on the beaches.

Naval support ships began pre-landing bombardment of the beaches at 05.30 hrs, from a range of some 1000 yards. The bombardment was lifted at 07.50 to allow carrier-borne aircraft to strafe the beaches in advance of the first landing waves, the naval bombardment moving on to inland targets. To further protect the assault waves, they were screened from the Japanese on the high ground to the north of the airfield by the firing of white phosphorous smoke shells. According to the plan, the first assault waves would be in Amtracs with subsequent support waves transferring at the edge of the reef from LCVPs to the Amtracs returning from the beaches. This mirrored in essence the plan for Tarawa in 1943, recalling thoughts of comrades in the 2nd Marine Division who had been forced to wade for several hundred yards, under murderous fire, to the beaches as some Amtracs did not survive to make the return journey. At Peleliu, the first waves were to be preceded by armoured LVTs (Amtanks). These Amtanks were Amtracs fitted with additional armour and 37mm gun turrets or 75mm

Howitzers and would serve as amphibious tanks to provide armour support for the initial assault waves until the tanks could be landed.

Also in advance of the first assault waves would be 18 landing craft (LCI) which were equipped with 4.5inch rocket launchers, each of which fired 72 rocket salvos onto the beaches. After the third assault wave had passed them, they would retire to the flanks to deliver fire when called upon. Four further LCIs were equipped with 4.2inch mortars and, standing off the northern part of White Beach, fired salvos continuously into the area inland from White Beach.

Whilst Oldendorf had confidence in the pre-assault bombardment, this would prove to be misplaced as it became obvious as the LVTs crossed the line of departure to make for the beaches that there remained many live Japanese on Peleliu. A number of Amtracs suffered direct hits from artillery and mortar fire, the smoke from this combining with that from the burning Amtracs and the smokescreen to obscure the beachhead from the advancing assault waves and the transports offshore.

An account of the following events, written by Sterling Mace, a BAR (Browning Automatic Rifle) man in K company, 3 Battalion/5th Marines (K-3-5) describes in almost surreal terms how young men respond to the ferocity of an assault on a heavily defended beach. Incidentally, Mace was in the same company as, among others, Eugene Sledge (see Eugene's book 'With the Old Breed' at Peleliu and Okinawa') and was in one of the first waves on Beach Orange 2. He wrote the following account 20 years after D-Day:

"Into the ship's hold we descended to find the amphibian tractors waiting with their diesel engines roaring. The sound was deafening. The smell of the acrid fumes was sickening. The noise of the engines, men and equipment reverberated off the steel hull. We huddled, thirty-six men and a 37mm field piece to a tractor, waiting for the bow doors to open. Suddenly, the doors opened wide letting the dawn's light shed on us. Out the bay doors poured the 'Alligators' which was a nickname for the amphibian tractors. One after another they splashed into the sea and, in full throttle, left the LST behind in its wake. I couldn't give you a count on the amount as I was not in a position to look over the bulkhead of the tractor I was in. We were jammed elbow to elbow. Not to mention the rise and fall of the waves. It seemed as if the Alligators were like rubber balls bobbing up and down in the ocean swells. As we rode up one crest I caught a glimpse of several sailors on board the LST drinking from coffee mugs and watching us depart. I thought, then, maybe I was in the wrong service. But looking at the faces of my buddies around me, I had mixed emotions. We had come so far together. I knew them. And to see their expressions of concern for themselves and each other, I was proud to be alongside of these men. Some were dead serious with furrows across their brow. Some were laughing and nervously joking. However, if the tractor made an uncommonly groan or hit a high peak of an underwater coral reef, the look of borderline panic would flush their faces.

The amphibians began to circle and gradually drawing closer to the island. The beach master was organizing the numerical order of the tractors for the different waves to land and follow the battle plan. The First Regiment was to land on our left. While the 7th would be on our right. The 5th would head straight, hitting Orange Beach 2. The beach was a little stretch of white sand with a backdrop of solid black smoke hiding the silhouette of tropical terrain of trees and mountains.

Off in the distance a flag is waved and the amphibians turn their course towards the short. Some 500 yards off shore were a line of LCIs launching 12,000 rockets onto the beach. The great battleships on the horizon are, also, firing away at the island. Someone in the outfit notices the tractor is fifteen yards in front of the main wave, which brings about a chorus of "slow down! You're going too fast". Nervous laughter.

There comes the sound of grating sand and coral from the bottom of the tractor. The rear door drops down and we exit. One after another we step out, turn to the right or left to run toward the beach ….."

Mace's feelings typified those of many Marines on D-Day. The first Marines to hit the beaches were men from the 3rd Battalion/1st Marines (3/1). They had landed on Beach White 1 at 08.32, only 2 minutes behind schedule, and were followed in the next 4 minutes by Marines on all 5 of the landing beaches. The Marines landed as planned on Beaches White 1 and 2, the 2nd Battalion on White 2 on the right and the 3rd on White 1 on the left, with the 1st Battalion as regimental reserve landing at approximately 09.45. On White 2 the 2nd Battalion/1st Marines (2/1) landed successfully and proceeded inland, the Japanese resistance being described in the after-action report as "moderate". The 2/1 pushed inland, support being provided from some of the armoured LVTs until their Sherman tanks were ashore. They gained a line approximately 350 yards inland through dense woodland by 09.30, however the progress of the hour had produced casualties. 2/1 halted at this point on the far side of the woods, facing the airfield and buildings and, tying in with the 5th Marines on their right flank, held until a solution could be found to the problems being encountered by the 3rd Battalion (3/1).

When 3/1 did hit beach White 2, they met stiff and violent opposition from the firmly-emplaced Japanese, with small arms fire immediately in front of them and artillery and mortar fire blanketing the entire beach area. As if this was not enough, lead elements of 3/1 had landed and advanced less than a hundred yards inland when they encountered a substantial natural obstacle in the shape of a coral ridge, almost 30 feet in height and which had not been shown on any map. The face of the ridge was a honeycomb of caves and firing positions blasted into the coral by the Japanese thereby creating superb defensive positions, which resisted all the initial assaults. The tanks which were brought in to support the assault troops in their attempt to take the northern part of the ridge blundered into a deep and wide anti-tank ditch and were pinned down for several hours under extraordinarily accurate enfilading fire.

Support for 3/1 was provided at first by Company A of the Regimental Battalion reserve (1/1), followed by Company B of the reserve following in the afternoon. Despite this, the gap which had opened up on the left could still not be closed. However a foothold was achieved in the south of the ridge later in the afternoon, alleviating the situation to a degree. But the seriousness of the situation remained, compounded by the news that 5 LVTs carrying the 1st Marines command group had been badly hit whilst crossing the reef; communications equipment and operators had both been lost. It was much later in the day that Divisional Command fully understood the precarious position in which the 1st Marines now found themselves.

More than 8 hours later, and following some of the fiercest fighting so far encountered in the Pacific, gaps in the 1st Marine lines were endangering the position of the entire Division on D-Day. Such was the danger that all available reserves were committed to the struggle, including Headquarters personnel and more than 100 men from the Engineer Battalion, who jointly formed a defence against the possibility of a Japanese counter attack which would engulf the whole line and onto the landing beaches. As luck would have it, the Japanese had not made plans for a counter-attack.

The Point, the ridge so christened by the Marines, could not be taken from the front and was eventually assaulted from the rear by units who had fought their way inland. Commanded by Captain George P Hunt, these units fought along The Point for almost 2 hours, neutralising enemy blockhouses and pillboxes along the way. The main defence installation, a reinforced concrete casement built into the coral and with a 47mm dual purpose anti-tank and anti-boat gun, with which they had raked the assault beaches all morning, was taken by Lieutenant William L Willis. Willis had attacked the installation from above, dropping a smoke grenade outside the blockhouse to camouflage the approach of his men and Corporal Anderson launched a rifle grenade through the firing aperture, disabling the gun and igniting the ammunition inside the blockhouse. The resulting explosion caused the remaining Japanese to flee the building, directly into the sights of the Marine riflemen awaiting their escape.

Captain Hunt and his remaining men – around 30 – remained stranded on The Point for 30 hours, suffering constant attack from the Japanese trying to exploit the gap in Company K's lines. When relief arrived, Hunt had only 18 men defending The Point and K Company had only 78 men out of the original 235.

On Beaches Orange 1 and 2 in the centre, the 5th Marines were doing a little better, the anti-boat fire on their way in being less effective, although they did suffer losses from artillery and mortar in assault boats and Amtracs. The 1st Battalion, 5th Marines (1/5) landed on Beach Orange 1 and the 3rd Battalion, 5th Marines (3/5) on Orange 2, both meeting scattered resistance on the beach and on their advance inland. Not for them the unmapped coral ridges as encountered by the 1st Marines; they advanced through coconut groves giving adequate cover and reached their objective line in front of the airfield, tying in with 2/1 on the left by 09.30.

Sterling Mace recalls a curious memory of Orange 2:

"There, as we're heading towards shore, a small dog is wagging its tail and barking at us. The sound of the dog's bark is suddenly unheard as the tractor's gunner opens fire. His fifty caliber machine gun blazing away at the vegetation along the beachfront. The last time we saw the dog, the little guy was in a mad dash down the beach....

In the time it took from the amphibian tractor in the surf, to the beach, everything was in mass confusion."

1/5 halted here, partly due to the lack of progress by the 1st Marines on the far left against The Point and partly due to the murderous Japanese artillery and mortar fire sweeping the airfield and the open ground in front of them. 3/5 on Orange 2 fared less well than 1/5 on Orange 1. Major Robert Ash, Commander Lieutenant Colonel A C Shoftner's executive officer, was lost within a few minutes of landing, the LVT carrying most of the Battalion's communications equipment and personnel being destroyed on the reef.

In accordance with the plan, I company and K company landed on the left and right respectively, L company following on closely as Battalion Reserve. I company were successful in making contact with 1/5 and they advanced inland together. The going was not as smooth however for K company, who encountered problems when sections of the 7th Marines landed on Orange 2 and not Orange 3 as per the plan. There was confusion on the beach which now delayed K company's advance and they did not line up with I company until 10.00 hrs.

The advance inland resumed at 10.30hrs but the 3rd Battalion's situation worsened. This was due in part to K company's advance route being through dense scrub which, although giving cover from Japanese shelling, meant that they started to move ahead of I company, eventually losing contact with them. Efforts were made to close the gap using L company, however the front line was stretched precariously for most of D-Day. Even when the Regimental Reserve, 2/5, landed in the afternoon and relieved I company, who then were to go around L company to tie in with them and K company, the confusion remained due to the inferior quality of maps of the area. The 3rd Battalion's bad luck continued with the command post being struck by a Japanese mortar barrage around 17.00hrs, Colonel Shofner being wounded and consequently evacuated, severely disrupting the 3rd Battalion's effectiveness. The Executive officer of the 5th Marines, Lt Col Lewis W Watt, took command of the Battalion but at this late hour in the day darkness had fallen before he had located the first of his companies and in fact it took all night to regain even a modicum of order.

So, by the end of D-Day, the front of the 5th Marines had three Battalions facing east, north and south with the 2nd and 3rd Battalions essentially back to back. Strange as this would seem, together they provided sufficient defence for the coming night.

The 7th Marines were to land on Orange 3 Beach with 2 Battalions in column and the remaining Battalion, 2/7, kept afloat as divisional reserve. The 3rd Battalion landed first, the 1st Battalion following shortly after. Obstacles on the reef, both natural and man-made, caused the Amtracs to approach the beach in a column, slowing down the attack and providing an easy target for the Japanese, who rained anti-boat fire onto them from Ngarmoked island to the south-west of the landing beaches, adding to the artillery and mortar fire from inland on Peleliu. This combination caused several Amtrac drivers to veer to their left and land on Orange 2 instead of Orange 3 and creating the confusion that was experienced by 3/5. Land mines and barbed wire added to the complications for 3/7 and valuable time was lost in efforts to get the 7th Marines back on course.

The next obstacle in front of the 7th Marines was a large anti-tank ditch just inland of Orange 3, which again had not been shown on any maps, however it became very useful. The pilot of one of the observation planes during the landings had sent a report to Divisional HQ identifying the ditch, which did prove extremely useful for moving troops forward more safely and was a ready-made dugout for the Battalion Command Post (CP). The 3rd Battalion now advanced inland, K company on their right and I company to their left, linking in with 3/5 who were advancing inland from Orange 2. By 10.45hrs K company had advanced around 500 yards and on the way had captured a Japanese radio direction finder. However, I company encountered Japanese resistance and had been halted in the area of the Japanese barracks by a combination of blockhouses and gun emplacements. They remained here awaiting tank support which was in fact operating in the wrong area due to a bizarre confusion of events. The two assaulting regiments centre and right were both part of the 3rd (3/5 and 3/7) and both had identical company identifications (I, K and L), hence the tank commanders looking for 3/7, who had strayed into 3/5 due to the anti-tank ditch on Orange 3 and other obstacles, when enquiring if they had found I company, third battalion, were told that yes they had. These troops were in fact I company 3/5 and not I company 3/7, but fortunately this would prove to be advantageous. This confusion resulted in a break in the two regiments, 3/5 pushing ahead whilst 3/7 paused to assess their situation. L company meanwhile were attempting to regain contact with 3/5 and pushing patrols further to the left until the foremost one reached the southern edge of the airfield, now outside the regimental action zone and several hundred yards rear of the units it was trying to reach.

1/7 had in the meantime landed on Orange 3 at 10.30hrs as planned, but some elements did end up on Orange 2. Whilst the original Japanese resistance was light, when the Battalion wheeled to the right as was the plan, it increased significantly. Again, the Marines were failed by inadequate maps, encountering a dense swamp that had not been shown on any map. The trail around this swamp, affecting the right half of the Battalion, was heavily defended and considerable time was spent in working around it, Colonel Gormley only confirming reaching the objective line at 15.20hrs. From this swamp the Japanese counter-attacked during the night, being repelled with assistance from black Marine shore party personnel who volunteered as riflemen.

General Rupertus, aboard the USS Dupage, was concerned at the lack of progress on the right and committed the divisional reconnaissance company ashore, later followed by an attempt to commit the divisional reserve. D-Day gains for the Marines were disappointing following the initial optimism. The 1st and 5th Marines fell well short of target, reasonable progress only being made by the 7th Marines. The gap in the centre of 3/5 on the left remained open, posing a threat to the entire south-facing line.

During the night, counter-attacks were overcome with relative ease, thanks to a combination of naval gunfire and star shells and the artillery of the 11th Marines. These attacks were coordinated and not the 'banzai' style attacks expected. One of the more major Japanese counter-attacks had been around 16.50hrs on D-Day, involving a tank-infantry sortie in the north of the airfield. The Marines were expecting an attack, particularly the 5th Marines facing onto the open ground in front of the airfield, and artillery, heavy machine guns and tanks had already been brought into that area by the regimental commanders.

The actions of the Japanese provided early indications of their intent – an increase in artillery and mortar fire, followed by an advance across the airfield by infantry. This was not the expected frenzied, drunken 'banzai' charge, rather a methodical, controlled advance of infantrymen. The formation of Japanese tanks with more infantrymen on the east of the ridges above the airfield had been spotted by a Navy aerial observer. These tanks moved forward, past the Japanese infantry who were advancing across the airfield and only 400 yards from Marine lines. For a short time, this looked as if it was going to be a serious and coordinated advance, but for some inexplicable reason the tank drivers set off at full speed towards the American lines, the infantry riding on them clinging on, and leaving their infantry way behind. There is no physical account of the following events. Remaining evidence suggests that there were between 13 and 19 tanks heading for the Marine lines, cutting diagonally in front of 2/1, who attacked them with flanking fire. Two of the tanks swerved off into the 2/1 lines and plunged over a coral embankment, crashing into a swamp. The crew members escaping from them were dealt with by the Marines. The remaining tanks, meanwhile, were under heavy fire from Marines of 1/5, the advancing Japanese infantry suffering fire and bombing from a Navy dive bomber.

As the tanks and their infantry passengers were annihilated, the Marine lines were closing behind them. Only two Japanese tanks escaped and numerous claims of confirmed hits were made by the Marines. It is unclear whether any of the infantry survived or whether they fled in the face of the tank support being destroyed.

There were several smaller counter-attacks along the line during the afternoon of D-Day, only one of which was of any substance. At 17.30hrs infantry supported by two tanks, which may have been the two that escaped earlier, attacked the lines of the 1st and 5th Marines. Both tanks were destroyed, the Japanese infantry did not reach the Marine lines.

The Marines observed that these counter-attacks were more coordinated and organised and not the suicidal Banzai charges of previous encounters, heralding a change in tactics against the Marines on Peleliu.

Crews of a US battleship's 20mm and 40mm guns take a breather, during the landings on Peleliu, 15 September 1944. (*USNHHC*)

Smoke and dust rises from the Peleliu shore, during the final stages of the pre-invasion bombardment, 15 September 1944. Photographed from an LCI gunboat, whose bow 40mm gun is visible in the foreground. Note waves breaking on the offshore reef. (*USNHHC*)

LTV assault waves approaching "White" and "Orange" landing beaches on the South-West side of Peleliu Island, 15 September 1944. Beach "White One" and "White Two" are in center, with "Orange" beaches beyond. Smoke from pre-invasion bombardment and possibly defending Japanese gun fire shrouds the scene. Part of the Japanese air field is visible in top left center. Photograph taken from a USS *Pennsylvania* (BB-38) plane. Note reef line offshore. (*USNHHC*)

The first wave of LVTs move toward the invasion beaches, passing through the inshore bombardment line of LCI gunboats, 15 September 1944. Cruisers and battleships are bombarding from the distance. The landing area is almost totally hidden in dust and smoke. Photographed from a USS *Honolulu* (CL-48) plane. (*USNHHC*)

Pacific Fleet landing craft launch a rocket attack against the beaches prior to landings by First Marine Division, 15 September 1944. Note: SH-LCI (R) 77. SH-LCI (G) 78 (in background).. (*USNHHC*)

First division Marines head for the beach, as their LVTs churn past the offshore line of LCI gunboats, 15 September 1944. Note gunner saluting from the LVT (2) in the foreground. Nearest LCIG is USS LCIG-452. An Idaho-class battleship is bombarding in the left distance. (*USNHHC*)

LCI gunboats move in on the beach area, during the final stages of the pre-invasion bombardment, 15 September 1944. Two PCs have taken position nearer shore, probably to act as landing craft guides. Several battleships and cruisers are firing in the distance. Nearest ship is USS LCIG-77. (*USNHHC*)

USS *Robinson* (DD-562) fires 40mm guns to cover underwater demolition team men clearing beach obstacles in mid-September 1944, prior to landings by the First Marine Division. (*USNHHC*)

The loss of USS *Noa* on 12 September 1944. USS *Fullam* (DD-474) recovers *Noa*'s survivors as USS *Honolulu* (CL-48) stands by in the background, in the morning on 12 September 1944. *Noa* sank after being rammed by USS *Fullam* (DD-474) while both were en route to the invasion of Peleliu. (*USNHHC*)

Casemate gun crew on USS *Mississippi* loading their 5/51 gun, during the bombardment of Peleliu, circa mid-September 1944. Note line of shell passers in the background, and the gun's breech in the lower right foreground. (*USNHHC*)

USS *Robinson*, a destroyer of Admiral Halsey's Third Fleet slips along the beach at Peleliu in the Palau group on D-Day, September 15, 1944. Its turrets trained land-ward, gun crews and lookouts eagerly scan the beach for a Japanese pill box or gun position to blast at almost point blank range. (*USNHHC*)

Underwater Demolition Teams. A massive wall rises from the water off Peleliu as 8,000 pounds of tetrytel explode. (*National Museum of the US Navy*)

U.S. Marines land on southwest pacific island of Peleliu. Troops of U.S. First Marine Division storm ashore from beached, amphibious tractors in an assault on Peleliu Island, in the Palau group of the southwest Pacific on September 14, 1944. Smoke from a burning tractor rises behind them. Overcoming strong Japanese opposition, the Marines within two days landed reinforcements and captured an important airfield. By September 21, the U.S. forces controlled all but a small northern strip of the island, which has a useful harbor. The Palaus are only 500 miles east of the Philippines. This image is a radiophoto sent from Honolulu to the U.S. Office of War Information. (*National Museum of the US Navy*)

Battle of Peleliu, September–November 1944. Underwater Demolition Teams. While members set their charges in the water of Peleliu, Palaus, a lookout keeps in touch with supporting warships, directing covering fire to blanket Japanese shooting at the swimmer. (*National Museum of the US Navy*)

Survivors of USS Noa (APD-24) sunk near Peleliu after being rammed by *Fullam* on September 12. As seen from USS *Indianapolis* (CA 35), September 15, 1944. At the extreme right the Executive Officer is interviewing one of the survivors. (*National Museum of the US Navy*)

Battle of Peleliu, September–November 1944. African-American Marines lying low on a typical beach scene moving forward. Photographed September 15, 1944. (*National Museum of the US Navy*)

Battle of Peleliu. Marines held down by sniper fire, September 15, 1944. (*National Museum of the US Navy*)

On board USS *Wayne* (APA 54) and bound for a hot landing on Peleliu Island, September 1944. (*National Museum of the US Navy*)

Marines of the first wave going ashore on D-Day on Peleliu. (*National Museum of the US Navy*)

The skies are blackened with smoke from the combined Naval and aerial bombardment of the Peleliu beach in the Palau Islands as land craft scurry shoreward with Marines. (*National Museum of the US Navy*)

Invasion of Peleliu, 15 September 1944. Original caption titles this photograph as, "Hot Java off Peleliu". Members of anti-aircraft gunnery crew on a US Navy LCI supporting the landing on the island on D-Day. Note, the battle raging on in the background while they take a dipper of hot coffee. (*National Museum of the US Navy*)

As supporting naval and air units pave the way with high explosives, Marine-laden assault craft form the first wave and move in for the attack on Peleliu. (*USMC Archives*)

US Marines on Orange Beach during the Peleliu landings. (*USMC Archives*)

An amphibious tractor burns on the beach as 1st Division Marines take shelter under a DUKW, Peleliu, September 1944. (*NARA*)

Marine with a radio on the beach. (*NARA*)

Donald Mellins served in Company E, 2d Battalion, 1st Marines during the Second World War. On 15 September 1944, he was killed in action while helping to repel an enemy tank attack on the island of Peleliu. (*USMC Archives*)

Japanese Type 95 Ha Go light tank from the 14th Infantry Division. It was destroyed by US Marine anti-tank teams on Peleliu in September 1944 during the famous Japanese counter-attack across the airfield. (*NARA*)

Marines on Beach, 1st. Div. 5th Marines Co. "A". Peleliu. (*NARA*)

A US Marine Corps LVTA4, D12 named *Lady Luck*, on Peleliu. (*Historic Military Press*)

1st Division Marines advancing inland from White Beach. (*Historic Military Press*)

The landings underway, 15 September 1944. (*NARA*)

The wreckage of a Japanese aircraft and a knocked-out tank pictured after the fighting around Peleliu airfield. (*NARA*)

A DUKW lies smouldering on the beach at Peleliu after taking a hit from indirect fire on 15 September 1944. (*NARA*)

Japanese anti tank ditch made an excellent location on Orange Beaches 1 and 2 for command posts for both the 5th and 7th Marines on D-Day. Brigadier General O P Smith used this ditch for advance Divisional CP on D-Day and it was the first CP location for Major General Rupertus when he arrived on D-Day +1.

Support waves of Marines huddle down in their Higgins boat awaiting transfer to the beaches by Amtrac or DUKW on D-Day

Several new innovations were tried out for the first time at Peleliu. Here pontoons with crawler cranes mounted lift landing craft over the coral reef in an effort to speed up the supply of much needed ammunition, water and medical supplies

An LVT(A)4 Amtank leaves its LST mother ship en route to take up position at the Line of Departure on D-Day

Navy Seabees begin to clear the landing beaches of all sorts of detritus left behind from disabled LVTs and DUKWs onto hand carts

A Navy Seabee dozer pulls one of the newly-designed amphibious trailers, first used at Peleliu. The trailers were pulled by Amtrac or DUKW to the beach from the coral reef

After the Japanese tank led counter attack on the afternoon of D-Day. The Japanese tanks and infantry advanced across the airstrip but were no match for the waiting Marine heavy weapons and Sherman tanks

Disabled Amtracs and DUKWs litter the beaches. The Japanese had the beaches and lagoon zeroed in and took a heavy toll of the first waves of assault troops

The Japanese had guessed where the Americans would land and as such had sown the lagoon and beaches with mines. Here a Navy demolition man tackles one of many mines on the beach

Disabled DUKWs and LVTs litter the beaches and lagoon. The DUKW in the foreground had detonated a mine on the beach

D-Day, Peleliu. Men of the 1st Marines use a disabled LVT (A)-4 for cover from murderous fire on White Beach 2

D-Day, Peleliu. In the lagoon of White and Orange beaches many Amtank, Amtrac and DUKWs can be seen burning, hit before they reached the beaches. Further out, troop-carrying Higgins Boats head inland but have to wait at the barrier reef to transfer to LVTs. In the distance the all-important airfield can be seen.

D-Day, Peleliu. Preceding the first assault waves Landing Craft, Infantry (Gun), LCI (G) each equipped with 72 no. 4.5inch rocket launchers, plaster the landing beaches.

D-Day, Peleliu. Smoke from fires from the earlier bombardment rise up from the airfield inland of the White and Orange beaches.

D-Day, Peleliu. Thick black smoke from the pre-landing bombardment obscures Peleliu beaches from the approaching Marines

D-Day, Peleliu. Amtanks, LVT (A) I s and LVT (A)4s of the 3rd Armoured Amphibious Tractor Battalion cross the barrier reef into the lagoon ahead of the troop-carrying Amtracs

D-Day, Peleliu. Pre-invasion bombardment continues ahead of the approaching waves of assault troops

D-Day. Amtanks (LVT(A)-4s) head for the beaches preceding the troop-carrying Amtracs.

D-Day Peleliu. Troop-carrying Amtracs head in to the landing beaches. Amtanks have already landed on the beaches ready to give fire support to the incoming assault troops.

Amtanks (LVT(A)-4) head for the invasion beaches obscured by smoke from the pre-landing bombardment

D-Day Peleliu. Troop-carrying Amtracs approach the landing beaches. Amtanks have already taken up firing positions on the beaches

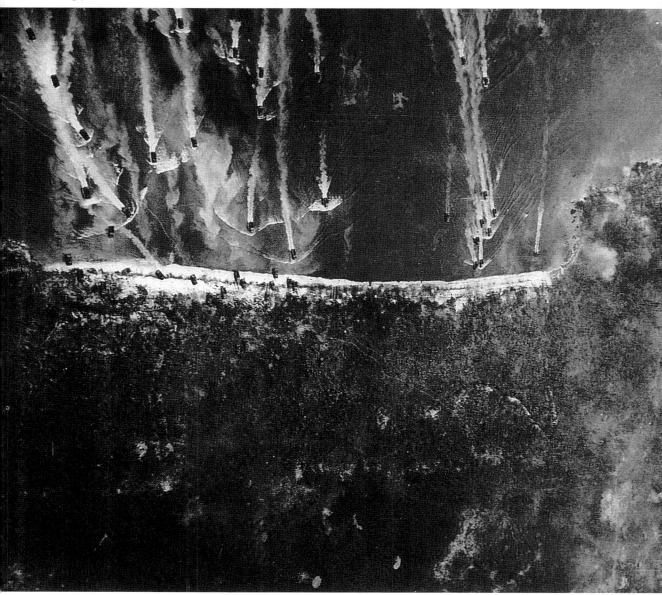

On D-day the Japanese counter-attacked with tanks supported by Infantry across the airstrip. This counter-attack was beaten back by the Marines; all but one of the Japanese tanks were destroyed

Going in, D-Day Peleliu. Amtracs loaded with infantry approach the line of departure. These Amtracs are still well out from the beaches as the Marines on board are still standing up

Aftermath of the Japanese tank/infantry counter attack in the afternoon of D-Day. Here one of 14 Type 95 Ha-Go tanks destroyed by Sherman tanks and Halftrack mounted 105mm guns

Remains of 2 of the 14 Ha-Go tanks destroyed during the failed Japanese counter attack on the afternoon of D-Day.

Aftermath of the failed Japanese counter attack across the airfield. Dead Japanese soldiers litter the perimeter of the airfield

Ha-Go tanks, destroyed by heavy weapons and Sherman tanks of the Marines on D-Day

USS Tennessee (BB-43) bombards Peleliu beaches prior to the assault troops landing

Three of the 14 Ha-Go Japanese tanks which led the Japanese counter attack across the airfield on the afternoon of D-Day. The counter attack failed dramatically, all but one of the 14 tanks being destroyed and the supporting infantry wiped out

D-Day, Peleliu. Higgins boats loaded with Marines wait at the 'line of departure' for the signal to advance to transfer their cargo of Marines into Amtracs at the barrier reef. Peleliu is almost totally obscured by thick black smoke from the pre-landing bombardments

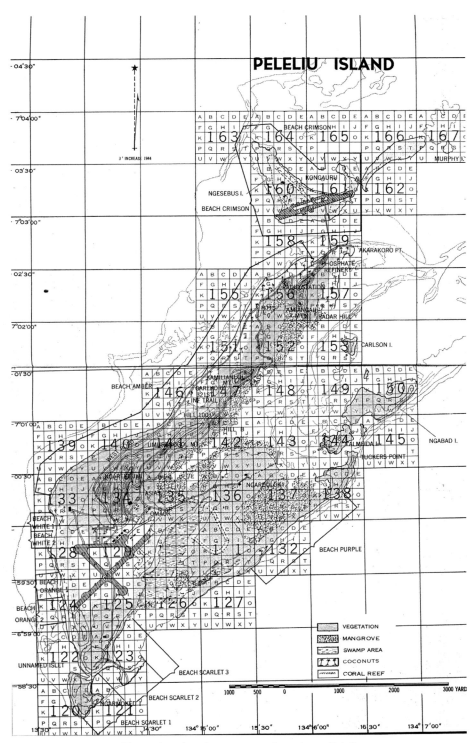

Target bombardment map of southern Peleliu

DUKWs were used to transport the wounded from aid stations first to waiting hospital ships and later to waiting C-46 Commando transport planes, as soon as the Seabees had the airstrip operational.

Chapter Four

D+1 To D+7 – The Nightmare Begins

General Rupertus and his staff landed on D+1, 09.50hrs, and commenced directing operations, taking over the command post set up by General O.P. Smith in the large tank ditch just inland from Orange 2 Beach on D-Day. With the area still under sporadic Japanese fire, this was an uncomfortable situation for Rupertus, his broken leg and ankle being still in a plaster cast.

Despite the D-Day objectives not being achieved and the 1st Marines on the left flank being in a serious situation, the plan continued to be based on the original battle plan for an advance across the island. On the right flank (to the south) the 7th Marines' objective was to advance east and south, whilst the 1st Battalion was anchored on Orange 3 Beach on the western shore and the 3rd Battalion was inland. The latter being hampered by a large Japanese blockhouse strongpoint which they had not overcome before nightfall on D-Day. The 3rd Battalion's (3/7) assault on the blockhouse resumed at 08.00, assisted by naval gunfire and tanks, however it was only finally reduced by a direct assault by demolitions teams under the cover of a smokescreen blanket. At around 09.25 hrs Company I reached the eastern shore and began digging in in case of Japanese counter landings.

Meanwhile, the 1st Battalion (1/7) had attacked in a southwards direction over "low and flat" terrain. This was how Intelligence described most of the Peleliu terrain. However, progress was hindered by the scrub overgrowth. The Japanese had anticipated this area to be a possible landing beach area and as such most of their defences faced seaward; 1/7 therefore were assaulting the defences from the flanks and rear, these being less protected. This whole area was a honeycomb of mutually supporting casements, blockhouses, bunkers and pillboxes, with trenches, rifle pits and well-cleared fields of fire. The going was difficult and deadly and it became clear that the Japanese were not going to give up easily, the Marines paying a high price for every inch gained on Peleliu. Supported by naval gunfire, air strikes, tanks and men from K Company (3/7), 1/7 pushed onwards, reaching the southern shore at approximately 10.25 hrs.

Natural factors also hampered progress for the Marines on Peleliu, with daytime temperatures in excess of 100°F aggravating the dehydration problem which, on top of the strain of protracted fighting, was beginning to tell on the Marines. The advance was suspended around noon for fresh supplies and water to be brought but unfortunately the 'fresh' water had been stored in 45 gallon oil drums which had not been thoroughly cleaned. The result was that the number of casualties created by this tainted water was more than that inflicted by the Japanese. The remainder of D+1 therefore was spent in bringing up supplies and tanks to assist in removing the Japanese defences and to cover the engineers clearing the numerous mines planted in the beach and sandpits by the Japanese. This was the only approach by land.

On D+2 the 7th Marines pushed further south to assault the south east and south west promontories on the southern shore. 3/7 were set to assault the south east promontory however the jump off was delayed until 10.00 following the discovery of yet another minefield which had to be cleared by the engineers. L Company then advanced, after an artillery and mortar barrage, supported by 3 tanks. A foothold was gained by 10.26 hrs and the area secured following fierce fighting, the promontory being taken by 13.20 hrs.

The south western promontory however was much larger than the south eastern one and was the target for 1/7, whose assault began at 08.35hrs, the Marines meeting stiff resistance from the outset. Their progress was paused to allow tanks and armoured LVTs to be brought up and for artillery to pound Japanese defences. The attack then resumed at 14.30hrs. They were successful in taking the Japanese first line of defence and although progress was slow and resistance stiff, half of the promontory was in Marine hands by nightfall on D+2. During that night additional armour was brought up and at 10.00hrs on D+3 the assault re-commenced. Progress was, as before, slow, many reserve elements suffering Japanese attack from caves and underground emplacements. Elements of A and C companies reached the southern shores at 13.44 hrs, but the area assaulted by B Company remained heavily defended. The tank support had been withdrawn to re-arm and B company were unable to resume their attack until assistance came from a bulldozer, which removed gun-mounted half tracks that had become bogged down. Explosions could be heard in the area of the Japanese defences and it became clear that the last few Japanese defenders had finished the job started by the Marines, the last few leaping from cliff tops into the sea and being picked off by Marine riflemen.

The taking of the two promontories secured the southern part of Peleliu and 1/7 and 3/7 prepared for a well-earned rest, Headquarters reporting "15.20 hrs D+3, 7th Marines mission on Peleliu completed." Sadly, not the case.

Whilst the 7th Marines were securing the south successfully, the 5th Marines in the centre were preparing to capitalise on their initial D-Day gains, the plan being to push east across the airfield on D+1 and swing round to the north east, the left flank of the 1st Marines being the pivot. It took just a little more than an hour for 1/5 to sweep the entire northern area of the airfield, the only significant resistance being from a series of emplacements in the hangar area. The area was secured by the late afternoon of D+1 after heavy fighting. The front line then had to be pulled back to a large anti-tank ditch for the night.

In the meantime, 2/5 were advancing on the right flank of 1/5 although progress was slow on open ground and with heavy Japanese resistance. On the east of the airfield the woodland gave way to a mangrove swamp, both heavily protected by Japanese emplacements; these were only overcome by hand-to-hand fighting and at a heavy cost. However, 2/5 had reached and connected with 1/5 by nightfall, in readiness for the advance the next day.

The advance of both 2/5 on the left and the 7th Marines on the right, 3/5 was virtually pincered out of the operations on D+1 and now concentrating on securing positions on the shoreline and giving assistance as much as was possible to 2/5 and 3/7. Colonel Watt, in temporary command of 3/5, returned to his post of Regimental Executive Officer, 5th Marines, after being replaced by Major John H Gustafson.

On D+2 the 5th Marines began advancing to the north east, coming under flanking fire from Japanese positions on the high ground in front of the 1st Marines. 1/5 achieved their objectives by mid-morning on D+2 and held until relieved by 3/5, who then took over the advance during the afternoon, before being pinned down by heavy flanking fire to their left. 2/5 on the right had more success, the woodland providing concealment from Japanese artillery and mortar fire. Although resistance on the ground was light, allowing 2/5 to advance beyond their objective, the Marines were suffering from the heat and difficult terrain, making frequent stops. Despite these obstacles, 2/5 had tied in with 3/5 on their left and the shoreline on their right by the end of D+2.

D+3 – 18 September – the 5th Marines were making continued progress, albeit slowly. The regimental boundary on their left was the road skirting the high ground of the Umurbrogol mountains, which had proved so problematic for Puller's 1st Marines. To the right, however, conditions were very different. With jump off at 07.00 hrs, 2/5 had hacked through dense jungle scrub whilst encountering only occasional resistance and had reached within two hours a road heading eastwards towards the shores of the island's north eastern peninsula. The road was bordered closely by swamps, reducing it to more of a causeway and creating a perilous journey for an advancing party. An advance patrol was sent ahead of the main body and an air strike called when they did not draw fire; the remainder could then advance in comparative safety. Unfortunately the air strike missed the target completely and an artillery barge was called in, following which elements of G and F companies started to cross the causeway. An unexpected air strike then strafed the advancing Marines, causing 34 casualties from 'friendly fire'.

In spite of these problems, and further casualties caused by misplaced 'friendly' artillery and mortar fire, the bridgehead was finally established and Regimental HQ now shifted 3/5 eastwards across the causeway to assist 2/5. Company L was tied in with the 1st Marines. By nightfall on D+3 there was a bridgehead north and east facing the main Ngardololok installations. This area was referred to in Marine documents and maps as the "RDF area", due to the presence of a Japanese radio direction finder.

D+4 – 2/5 and 3/5 advanced on the RDF area, meeting only light resistance from the Japanese stragglers, many of whom had elected to hide and not fight. Both Battalions pressed on, 3/5 reaching the eastern shoreline and later the southern shores (American designation Purple Beach) by the end of the day. They went on to secure the whole peninsular by D+6, whilst 2/5 had continued east and north, stopping short of the small island just off the causeway, Island A, which had been checked and found to be deserted by a patrol sent over on D+5. They pushed further north, again without meeting opposition, to a second, larger island – Ngabad.

D+8 – 23 September. G company secured a small island, which was unnamed and undefended, just north of Ngabad, which completed the 5th Marines' original mission on Peleliu. However, on the Division's left flank things were not going quite as well.

From their start on D-Day, Puller's 1st Marines had come up against intense and well-coordinated resistance from Japanese defence in the Umurbrogol mountain region.

On D+1 Rupertus had ordered the Division reserve (2/7) to be transferred to the strained 1st Marines to "maintain momentum" – as he would repeat to Puller many times! Also on D+1, 2/1, initially facing east, swung left (north), intending to take the built up area between the airfield and the mountains. They crossed the airfield within half an hour in their achievement of this goal. However, on the left the 3rd Battalion could not advance at all, the regimental reserve 1/1 being called in to assist during the afternoon. A 500 yard segment of the ridge was captured by Marine infantry and tank support following bitter fighting and B company was now able to make contact with K company, the latter having been isolated for around 30 hours. The ferocious Japanese counter attack during the night of D+1 was repelled, but the hard fighting had taken a toll, leaving K Company with only 78 of its original 235 men by the morning of D+2 and resulting into the Company being ordered into reserve.

By D+2 the 1st Marines, having already suffered more than 1,000 casualties, saw their combat teams assembled in line on the regimental front, with 3/1 on the left flank, 1/1 in the centre and 2/1 on the right flank. The newly-arrived 2/7 was in reserve.

On D+2 elements of the 1st Marines witnessed for the first time the Umurbrogol mountains, the aerial photographs doing no justice to their true nature, described in a later 1st Marines narrative as:

"a contorted mass of coral, strewn with rubble, crags, ridges and gulches."

2/1 were first to encounter the defences of the Umurbrogol, their initial progress being interrupted by the first of the many ridges; they christened this one Hill 200. The slopes of Hill 200 were scaled, with much bitter hand-to-hand fighting and heavy casualties, but by nightfall the crest was secured. The Marines could not rest on their laurels, however, as they immediately came under fire from Hill 210 (the next ridge) and so the pattern was set.

1/1 were progressing well when they came upon an unmarked blockhouse, which Admiral Oldendorf had reported as destroyed in the pre-invasion bombardment. However, it was only destroyed when fire from naval 14 inch guns was called upon, directly onto the emplacement.

3/1 on the left had a little better fortune, being able to advance along the relatively flat coastal plain; however they had to call a halt when in danger of losing contact with 1/1 on the right flank.

D+3 – Puller was being urged on by divisional command, although by now his 1st Marines had suffered 1,236 casualties. All available reserves, including pioneers, engineers and headquarters personnel now became infantrymen and 1/1 went into reserve and were replaced by 2/7. D+3 and many more became an exact repetition of D+1. Hill 210 was taken by 2/1, but the Japanese counter attacked Hill 200, forcing the Marines' withdrawal. This situation became so desperate by the afternoon that B Company, 1/1, who had just gone into reserve, were now sent to assist 2/1 in the assault of yet another ridge, Hill 205, which turned out to be isolated. B Company now pressed on but were pushed back by defences which later became known as the "Five Sisters". Once again, 3/1 on the left fared well and advanced along the coastal plains, pausing to maintain contact with 2/7 in the centre.

D+4 – following a night of persistent harrowing counter attacks, the remainder of the 1st Marines plus 2/7 resumed the attack following a naval and artillery barrage. Again, the best progress was achieved on the left, 3/1 pushing onward but again being forced to halt. 2/7 in the centre trudged from ridge to ridge, suffering heavy casualties, whilst 2/1 on the right pressed on over similar terrain meeting stiff resistance, which increased with each successive ridge. Although 2/1 were unaware, their current attack was against what would later be known as the final Japanese pocket in the Umurbrogol mountains.

At the end of D+4 the 1st Marines existed in name only; they had suffered more than 1500 casualties.

D+6 – III Amphibious Corps commanding General, Roy Geiger, visited Puller following yet another day of bitter hand-to-hand fighting. Seeing face to face the condition of Puller and his men, on his return to Divisional Headquarters Geiger conferred with Rupertus and some of his staff. Following an acrimonious argument, Geiger ordered Rupertus to replace the 1st Marines with the 321st RCT of the 81st Army Division who were currently on Angaur. Puller and his men were to be sent back to the divisional rear base, Pavuvu. By this time the 1st Marines had reported 1749 casualties. The fierce fighting in the Umurbrogol which had reduced the 1st Marines to this state was later described by one Marine as:

> "I picked up the rifle of a dead Marine and I went up the hill; I remember no more than a few yards of scarred hillside, I didn't worry about death anymore, I had resigned from the human race. I crawled and scrambled forward and lay still without any feeling towards any human thing. In the next foxhole was a rifleman. He peered at me through red and painful eyes. I didn't care about him and he didn't care about me. As a fighting unit, the 1st Marines was finished. We were no longer human beings, I fired at anything that moved in front of me, friend or foe. I had no friends, I just wanted to kill".

Goodyear FG-1 "Corsair" fighter (BuNo 14513) (F4U-1A) lands on Peleliu airfield just two weeks after the invasion of the island in September 1944. Plane is probably from a Marine squadron, and appears to be carrying a Napalm tank. A Curtiss R5C-1 transport plane is in the background. (USNHHC)

View taken on 19 September 1944, showing a Convair OY-1 Grasshopper being manhandled on the flight deck of USS Petrof Bay (CVE-80), during the Peleliu Operation, codename Operation *Stalemate II*. Note motto on cowling: "It flies, don't it?" (*USNHHC*)

African-American attendants of GROPAC-9 medical department relaxing after a hard day's work. (*National Museum of the US Navy*)

Battle of Peleliu, September–November 1944. Lieutenant Junior Grade John J. Malone, USN, Catholic Chaplain with the Seventh Regiment of the First Marine Division says mass on Peleliu Island for the Marines who fell while storming the island. Comrades of the dead fighters kneel in prayer. (*National Museum of the US Navy*)

Sailors and Seabees unloading fuel from small landing craft at beach, September 15, 1944. (*National Museum of the US Navy*)

Battle of Peleliu, September–November 1944. Admiral Cochran and party at First Division rear CP with Lieutenant Colonel J.W. Ross, Executive Officer. (*National Museum of the US Navy*)

Battle of Peleliu, September–November 1944. Group of Afro-American Marines acting as stretcher bearers for the 7th Marines. (*National Museum of the US Navy*)

Battle of Peleliu, September–November 1944. These Marines are from Youngstown, Ohio, Pittsburgh and Philadelphia, Pennsylvania. They are on Peleliu Island and acting as stretcher bearers. They have just returned from the front lines and are catching a couple of minutes rest before returning to the lines. (*National Museum of the US Navy*)

Battle of Peleliu, September–November 1944. Seabees, members of the shore party group, are shown loading gas and oil on beach. Photographed by Fitzgerald, October 1944. (*National Museum of the US Navy*)

Airstrip on Peleliu Island, Palau Islands showing bomb craters, September 14, 1944. (*National Museum of the US Navy*)

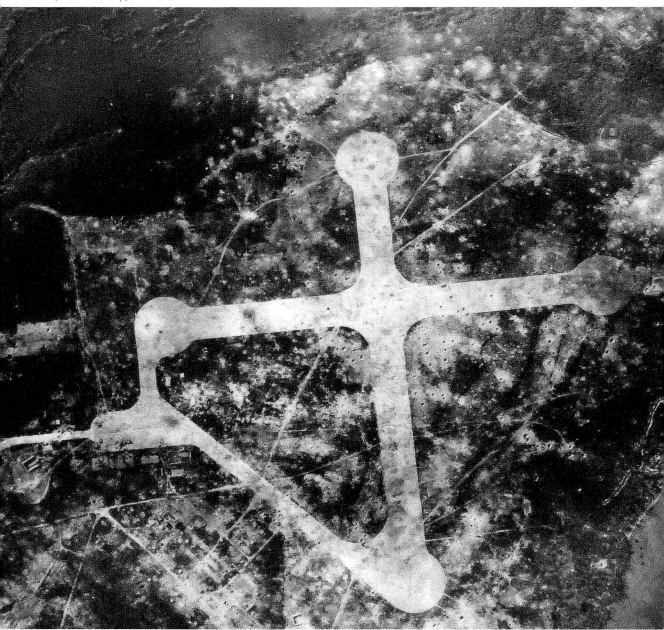

Marine firing a Tommy Gun at the Japanese from a sand bank on Peleliu, 29 September 1944. (*National Museum of the US Navy*)

USS LST 661 beached by the heavy surf and Navy tugs are trying to free it on Peleliu. (*National Museum of the US Navy*)

Chaplain Rufus W. Oakley holding services within a few hundred yards of Japanese positions, well within range of their mortars if they had chosen to throw them. Peleliu, September 1944. (*National Museum of the US Navy*)

Marines support tanks, Peleliu, September 1944. Advance-After the beachhead had been established on Peleliu, the inland drive was under way. Here Marine infantrymen inch ahead on their bellies to support their tanks attacking Japanese strong points. (*USMC Archives*)

Lieutenant Colonel R.G. Ballance, Champagne, Ill., of the First Marine Division, resumes his duties as Commander of a Pioneer Battalion, despite shrapnel wounds received on the Peleliu beach. (*USMC Archives*)

Marines rest by a captured Japanese position. (*NARA*)

Marines pushing inland from the beaches. (*NARA*)

The aftermath of the landings at Peleliu on 15 September 1944. (*NARA*)

Marines during the fighting for Peleliu airfield. (*Historic Military Press*)

Marines pictured immediately prior to the assault on Japanese positions at Peleliu airfield. (*NARA*)

A war dog and handler from the 1st Marine Division on Peleliu, 15 September 1944. (*NARA*)

A battered Japanese bunker on Peleliu after its capture during the fighting in 1944. (*NARA*)

Typical surroundings around the Umurbrogol mountains after the Naval bombardment had stripped away all the foliage. The hard coral ground made digging foxholes impossible

Marines survey one of the Japanese gun positions littered with boxes of ammunition but no sign of the gun itself, possibly one of the 150mm mortars that wreaked havoc throughout the battle

Sherman tanks cross the airfield, The engagement between these Shermans and Japanese Ha-Go tanks was no match, the Shermans destroying all but two of the Japanese tanks in the afternoon of D-Day

Marine Sherman tanks used the airstrip initially to re-arm and fuel up – until the Seabees had the airstrip operational

D+1 – men of the 5th Marines begin to move out across the open airfield. They will receive murderous fire from the defending Japanese who are well dug in on the far side of the airstrip

Peleliu – with the invasion beaches secured, supplies of all kinds begin to arrive on the beaches. All supplies had to be transferred at the reef line into Amtracs until the Navy Construction Battalions (Sea Bees) constructed a causeway from the beaches to the reef line

With the airstrip in Marine hands the work of repairing it can begin. Barracks and administration buildings lay in ruins in the background, all were heavily defended by the Japanese.

Supplies of fuel and water in 45 gal drums are floated across the lagoon to the beach head. In time the SeaBees blasted holes in the barrier reef to allow landing craft to access the beaches

Several Japanese blockhouses had withstood the pre-invasion naval bombardment and slowed the advance inland. These blockhouses were only neutralised by targeted naval gunfire followed by assault by ground troops with tanks, flamethrowers and demolition charges.

Close order fighting among the ruins of the Japanese administration buildings on the north side of the airstrip

Corporal Peter P Zacharko stands by a captured Japanese 141mm mortar. These mortars rained shells onto the invasion beaches and inland as the Marines advanced

M3, 37mm anti-tank gun of the 5th Marines. A useful weapon against blockhouses and caves as well as against tanks. Note the Japanese concrete bunker relatively untouched by the pre-invasion bombardment

Japanese block house on the airfield on Peleliu. Relatively untouched by the pre-invasion bombardment. Blockhouses like this had to be taken out by satchel charges and flamethrowers

Marines of 2/1 advance through heavy scrubland now well blasted by the pre-assault bombardment heading for the airfield

Japanese machine gun and crew destroyed in the fighting for the airfield on D+1. Note prize Samurai sword in the hands of the Marine – "to the victor the spoils"

AFTER 3ᴿᴰ BANZAI CHARGE

Peleliu
AIR PORT
9-1

Marine Sherman tanks refuel and re-arm on the new captured airstrip on Peleliu. The Japanese Ha-Go tanks were no match for the Shermans on Peleliu

Sherman tanks lead the advance through the swampland south east Peleliu. Note disabled Sherman at the head of the causeway, knocked out by Japanese gunfire.

Remnants of 3/1 81mm mortars move forward D+3

Chapter Five

81st Infantry take Angaur and Ulithi

The 81st Infantry Division provided the Corps' reserve for Operation Stalemate II, available for use as and when required and then, when the situation on Peleliu was well in hand, to make an assault on Angaur. On 16 September – D+1 – the 1st Marine Division commander declared "Peleliu would be secured in a few more days", hence the assault on Angaur was scheduled for D+2 on Peleliu, ie 17 September.

The RCT322 landed on the east Red Beach and RCT321 on the south east Blue Beach as planned, following a pre-landing bombardment by the Navy. Both these RCTs came up against only light resistance from small arms and mortars on the beaches; they were pushing on inland soon after landing. However, the "Wildcats" became snarled up in the dense jungle rainforest, teeming with Japanese machine guns and snipers concealed in the trees. Their advance was slow and costly but as night fell both RCTs had reached their objectives, even if still separated by 1500 yards and each having to form their own perimeters due to the Japanese still occupying pockets of land. Night-time counter attacks by the Japanese also caused both RCTs to fall back, but were eventually repelled.

On the second day, following a three-hour long artillery bombardment, both the RCTs advanced in north and west directions, the right flank of RCT321 making contact with RCT322 and uniting the two advances. In spite of stiff resistance, by nightfall the left flank of RCT321 had pushed almost to the western shores, effectively dividing the island almost into two.

On the third day – 19 September – following a night of several small scale counter attacks by the Japanese, the RCT321 pushed onward, succeeding in dividing the island in two. They then wheeled to the left and pushed on down the south west of the island, stopping almost at the shoreline at nightfall. At the end of this third day only two areas remained in Japanese hands, the most significant being the north-east central area around Romauldo Hill, which consisted of a series of ridges similar to Peleliiu but fortunately not as vast.

As the situation on both Peleliu and Angaur was now well in hand, the Corps Reserve (81st third RCT –323) went on to their secondary target as planned – Ulithi Island.

On the fourth day RCT 321 successfully routed the last remaining Japanese on the west and went on to begin a similar exercise on the Ramauldo pocket. On the same day, Corps Commander General Geiger contacted the 81st Commander, General Mueller, regarding the provision of one RCT for immediate deployment to Peleliu. General Mueller detailed RCT321 for this duty as soon as they could be re-organised and so on 20 September the transfer to Peleliu began, leaving the RCT 322 to complete the task on the remaining Japanese defences on Angaur. General Mueller declared the island secure by 20 September, but it was not until 19 October that the RCT322 finally defeated Major Goto and his last remaining men.

In comparison to their casualties on Peleliu, those on Angaur were lighter with 260 killed, 1354 wounded and 940 incapacitated. In contrast, the Japanese had an estimated 1338 killed and 59 taken prisoner.

Thomas G Climie was a Sergeant in the 321st Reg, 81st Division and took part in the invasion of Angaur. His account is as follows:

"At Guadalcanal we had our last practice amphibious landing. We sailed from Guadalcanal on September 8, 1944, and now we were told we were going to have our first combat on Angaur and Peleliu of the Palau Islands. Now I am a very fussy and finicky eater, so I went to the ship's galley and asked the cooks if I could get some canned goods to go. Now most of the sailors were very good to Army men because they knew what we were going to have to endure. They told me to take what I wanted – if I didn't get caught and they would look the other way. So from time to time I took many cans of fruit juice, beans, canned pork, canned turkey etc; all of these were delicious. I filled two duffel bags with these. The night before we left the ship, one of my buddies said "Climie how about coffee?" I went back to the galley and asked. One of the cooks showed me the room where everything was stored. The 50-pound bags of coffee were way in the back, halfway down the aisle sleeping on a cot was the sailor who watched over it. I looked down the aisle at the coffee. The lights were out. I got the coffee, put it on my shoulder and on the way to the door I tripped on the guard's shoes. He awoke and yelled, but I was out of the door and long gone. The sailors gave me a rubber bag to put the coffee in to keep it dry. You will hear about my 3 bags of food off and on later.

Our convoy arrived in the Palau area on Sept 15, 1944. I saw 3 days of the heaviest shelling of Angaur and Peleliu that I have ever seen. Guns of all sizes from all the ships were bombarding the islands. The sky was full of planes strafing, bombing and releasing napalm fire bombs. The island couldn't be seen for fire and smoke. The first men reported all vegetation and buildings destroyed, but no bodies. The Japs were dug in and living in caves. On Peleliu, there was a thousand-man cave with many entrances and 6 stories high and with a complete hospital in it.

The Marines landed on Peleliu at 0832 September 15, 1944. We, the Wildcats, were to invade Angaur on September 16 and the night of the 15th the Navy gave us a huge farewell feast – steak, chicken, strawberries, ice cream etc. We were given candy, cigs, matches, ammo, etc to take ashore. Then our invasion of Angaur was changed to the 17th.

The morning of September 17, 1944, Fox Day, most of us said our prayers and waited. When we got the word, we went over the side, down the nets and into the landing craft. Some guys in our company had a small monkey and a chimp (the size of an 8 or 10 year old kid). They would climb and pass us on the ships landing nets like we were standing still. I was in the third wave, and this is something to remember – each wave of landing craft keeps going around in circles waiting for the word to go ashore. Men are crying, praying, some laughing. As our third wave started for shore, you would see the wrecked boats, tanks, DUKWs and shattered bodies all over the beach and in the water that is red from blood. My landing craft got near shore, the ramp came down and we stepped into the water. We were now on our own. We raced for shore going past floating dead bodies. I got ashore, found a shell hole and dove into it. There was machine gun fire, rifle fire, mortars, light artillery fire everywhere – everyone yelling and screaming.

We had landed on Blue Beach. I carefully worked my way inland taking advantage of any cover I could use, a rock here, a bush there. Believe me, I think I aged at least 10 years that day. As much as you prepare yourself, you cannot come near to reality.

The first night we had advance a little way from the beach. Four of us found another shell hole. We dug it bigger and deeper and prepared for the first night. We rigged up cans to bushes so we could hear if anything tried to get through. The officers, who always took their bars off during combat, told us not to be trigger happy on our first night.

A lot happened that first night. As it got dark, we took turns watching for the enemy. The other 3 would take off their helmets and try to sleep. No one had told us about the land crabs. They are hard shelled and the size of a pretty good dinner plate. Well, when the first one fell into the fox hole and landed on a helmet, you can imagine the noise. Four men jumped and had their rifles and bayonets ready. When we saw what it was we all laughed. Ask any Wildcat about the land crabs. While I was on watch, there was a bush in the distance and a light breeze blowing it. At times it looked like a Jap creeping up. I had my rifle with the safety off trained on it for 2 hours. We heard some of the cans rattle and I think everyone fired at it. I looked and saw a dog running with his tail wagging. I think he got through unhit. Finally, our first night was over and did everyone appreciate that old sun when it came up.

For four or five days on Angaur we suffered cuts from the coral rock, tearing of skin by the shrubbery and we had to literally blow the Japs out of their caves and pillboxes. Dirt, bullets flying everywhere – a nightmare for sure. Angaur was declared secured at 10.34 on September 20. We were proud of this – only 4 days, and the Marines were still in deep trouble on Peleliu. "

ANGAUR ISLAND

JAPANESE FORTIFICATIONS

AS OBSERVED THROUGH 25 AUGUST 1944

Army Amtracs carrying men of the 81st 'Wildcat' Division head into the landing beaches on Angaur,
17 September (D + 2 on Peleliu)

Aerial view of Angaur looking south-west from Beach Red, where the 322nd Infantry, 81st Division US Army landed on 17 September. (*US Navy*)

Major General Paul J Mueller, US Army, Commanding General 81st Infantry Division – "Wildcats". Mueller had commanded the "Wildcats" throughout training both on the US mainland and the Jungle Warfare School on Hawaii. Although lacking the 1st Marine Division's combat experience, Mueller was confident his men were ready for the task. Mueller would eventually take command of garrisoning Peleliu and of the 'mopping up' phase from the Marines

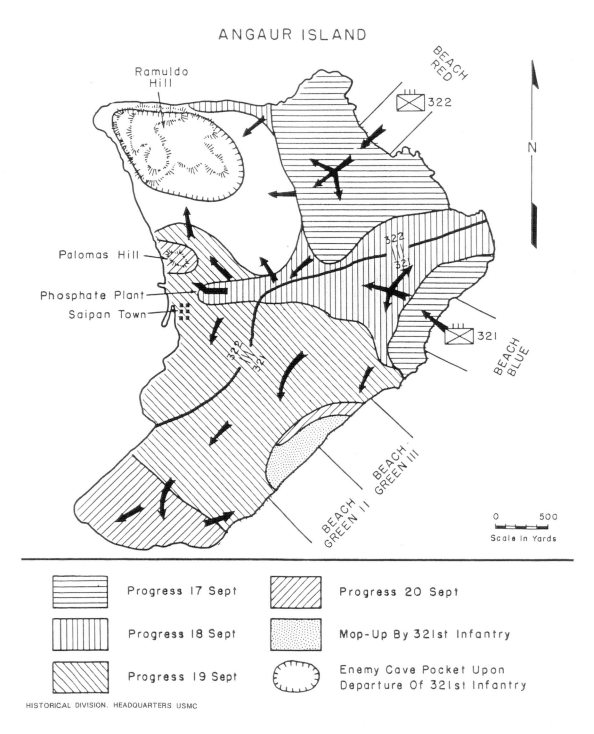

ANGAUR ISLAND

Ramuldo Hill

BEACH RED

322

N

Palomas Hill

Phosphate Plant

Saipan Town

322
321

322
321

321

BEACH BLUE

BEACH GREEN II

BEACH GREEN III

0   500
Scale In Yards

Progress 17 Sept

Progress 20 Sept

Progress 18 Sept

Mop-Up By 321st Infantry

Progress 19 Sept

Enemy Cave Pocket Upon Departure Of 321st Infantry

HISTORICAL DIVISION. HEADQUARTERS USMC

Angaur Island assault 17–21 September 1944.

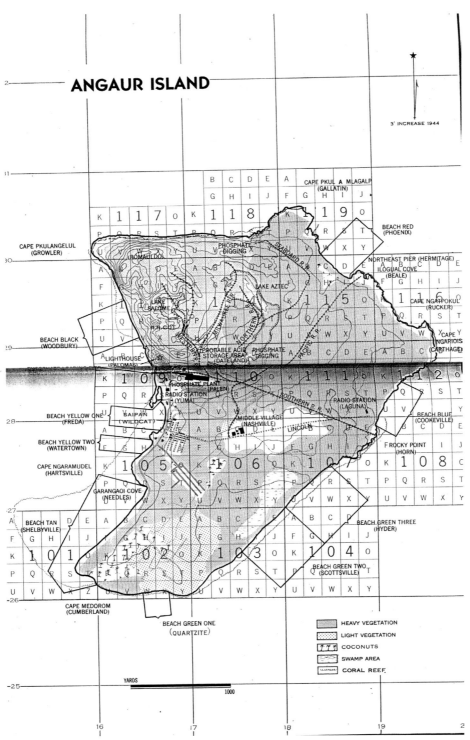

Target bombardment map of Angaur

Chapter Six

The Nightmare Continues.
D+8 – D+14

When it was discovered that the Japanese had attempted to reinforce the garrison on Peleliu on 23 September (D+8), barges were sent on two separate occasions from Koror and Babelthuap and on both occasions were intercepted by the Americans, even though one almost complete battalion did make it. It now became clear that securing northern Peleliu was more urgent than eradicating defences in the Umurbrogol mountains.

On 23 September, the 81st infantry's 321 RCT started to arrive from Angaur to replace the 1st Marines who were initially pulled back to the south of the island and eventually to Pavuvu. On 24 September (D+9) the 321 started the drive north eastwards along the coastal plain, with the aim of pushing past the Umurbrogol pocket with the 5th Marines and then on to northern Peleliu, the 7th Marines taking over the 1st Marine positions.

Due to the terrain it was impossible to use tanks or other vehicles and infantry troops had to clamber over coral and ridges in their efforts to protect the right flank. When the ridges were taken, vehicles would be able to use the east/west roads to bring supplies. These east/west roads were the major feature of the coastal plateau, running almost the full length of Peleliu. Although being the main route for the 321st's drive, it was dominated by coral protrusions and ridges which were still held by the Japanese, who rained murderous fire on anything that moved on the road.

The 321st had relieved the 3rd battalion/1st Marines (3/1) who had been tied in with 3/7 on the right flank. Orders were given for 3/7 to advance behind 2/321 on the high ground as the push to the north east was made. Rather than attacking the ridges as ordered, 2/321 chose to take the road, then reported that 3/7, who had been outpaced by 2/321 on the flat ground, were not keeping up. 3/7 were then ordered by Colonel Hanneken to capture the ridges which should have been the work of 2/321. This they did but not without cost, creating a strain on the relationship between the units. However, 321 pushed on and by D+10 the 5th Marines passed through them to make the final drive to the ruins of Garekoru village. During the afternoon on that day, 1/5 seized a radio station complex north of Garekoru, 3/5 taking the high ground on the right of 1/5. Although the Japanese defended as strongly as ever, some of the defenders were Navy construction units and not as highly trained. They were soon overcome by tanks, flamethrowers and demolition charges.

D+11 and D+12 saw full day fighting and small counter-attacks during the night. By the end of D+12, 2/5 had secured the northern shore – Akarakoro Point – and the Marines now held the area, although the Japanese still held it beneath ground. 2/5 now turned and attacked south to give support to 1/5 who were still labouring away at hills 1, 2 and 3 as well as radar hill on hill row. For the next two days the Marines fought determinedly to the top of hill row, leaving behind them many Japanese defenders who were now sealed in the caves.

Whilst 1/5 and 2/5 were battling on hill row, Marines of 3/5 made preparation for an amphibious assault on Ngesebus and Kongauru islands just off Akarakora point. Following a text book operation, 3/5 landed on Ngesebus following a massive bombardment by Navy ships and land-based artillery, Marine aircraft from VMF-114 out of Peleliu airstrip adding aerial support. 3/5 were able to go ashore with no casualties and took out all beach defences before proceeding to the ridges and caves further inland. By the end of D+13 most of the opposing force had been overrun with help from tanks and armoured LVTs.

By D+14 only the Umurbrogol pocket remained untaken.

The 'mopping up' operation began on D+14 and Ngesebus and Kongauru declared secure. The loss of 48 Marine casualties had cost Nakagawa 463 first rate troops over a period of 36 hours. 3/5 now went into divisional reserve after turning the islands over to 2/321.

Marines investigate a Japanese landing barge after attacking it with LVTs off Peleliu during the US invasion in September 1944. (*USNHHC*)

Peleliu under fire, probably during the pre-invasion bombardment, circa 12–15 September 1944. Photographed from USS Honolulu (CL-48) plane. Photo looks North-East, with the airfield in the foreground and Umurbrogol ridge in the distance, partly shrouded in smoke. (*USNHHC*)

Using a flame throwing amphibious tractor, Marines shoot a tongue of fire at enemy strong points in a cave-infested hillside on Peleliu. Six of these LVT-4s fitted with US Navy Mark I flame thrower were at the disposal of the Marine and Army units on Peleliu.

Battle of Peleliu, September–November 1944. Major General W. H. Rupertus, USMC, and Vice Admiral Cochrane, USN, and Colonel H.D. Harris, leave the Command Post after a conference. Note General Rupertus still needs to use a walking stick to support his leg and ankle injured during landing practise (*National Museum of the US Navy*)

Battle of Peleliu, September–November 1944. Skull and danger sign in combat area. (*National Museum of the US Navy*)

Warned! Warned by the large sign of the presence of sniper fire on this section of the Peleliu Island road, the Marines draw their pistols and assume an alert attitude as they go through the dangerous area. Sign reads, "Danger / Sniper Fire Along / Road Next Mile / Keep Moving / No Parking on the Road." Photographed October 12, 1944. (*National Museum of the US Navy*)

Tracking the Japanese on Peleliu in the Palau group, Private First Class John Clifton, Private First Class Anthony Tillman haul ammunition and cans of fresh water to combat troops busy on a hill ahead flushing the last Japanese out of their caves. Note the 1st Marine Division UNIS diamond marking on water can. (*National Museum of the US Navy*)

Invasion of Peleliu. Victim of Peleliu sniper. Members of a Marine demolition crew, assigned to blasting forward enemy positions on Peleliu in the Palau Islands, evacuate one of their comrades who was wounded by a Japanese sniper. Note the bullet hole in the steel helmet he is clutching. (*National Museum of the US Navy*)

U.S. Marine wounded in action at Peleiu, gets a drink of water from the canteen of a thoughtful buddy. (*National Museum of the US Navy*)

View from amphibious tank while crossing in third wave from Peleliu to Ngesebus. (*National Museum of the US Navy*)

A huge column of smoke rises skyward from an ammunition dump on Peleliu Island near the airport. R5D-1s on the airfield were hit during the fire, which was marked by numerous explosions. Photograph released 15 October 1944. (*National Museum of the US Navy*)

Private First Class Douglas Lightheart, USMC, right, cradles his 30 caliber machine gun in his lap, while he and his buddy Private First Class Gerald Churchby take time out for a cigarette, while mopping up the enemy on Peleliu Island. (*National Museum of the US Navy*)

Picking their way through the rocky terrain on Peleliu, a column of Marines moves up to the front lines. This is the type of terrain on which the Leathernecks battled the remnants of the Japanese forces on the island. (*USMC Archives*)

A handler of the Marine War Dog contingent participating in the Peleliu action, reads a note just delivered by his canine messenger. (*USMC Archives*)

Marines of the 1st Marine Division on Peleliu, 1944. (*NARA*)

Marines manning a 75mm Pack Howitzer, hurl shells at enemy ridge positions on Peleliu, from hastily-dug emplacements. (*USMC Archives*)

Mail, the number one morale builder, is delivered to Marine machine gunners in their position at the front lines on Peleliu. (*USMC Archives*)

A Corsair bombing Japanese positions on Peleliu. As a result of Maj Gayle's targeting of enemy positions in the Umurbrogol, napalm-laden Marine Corsairs lifted from Peleliu's airfield, and returned to the field to be rearmed, in perhaps the shortest wheels-down bombing run of the Pacific War. (*NARA*)

Tom Lea would call this 'The Thousand Yard Stare' a Marine that had been on Pelelia too long. (*NARA*)

Marines installing telephone lines under fire on Peleliu, September 1944. In the background is seen part of famous Bloody Nose Ridge, scene of the fiercest fighting on Peleliu. (*NARA*)

This dramatic time exposure made in 1944 records a fierce night assault by Japanese forces against U.S. Marines on Peleliu in the Palau Islands. Japanese forces were dug in behind Bloody Nose Ridge, visible below a night sky lit up by parachute flares. The long straight lines are tracer shells from Japanese gunners firing on Marine aircraft. At the right edge of the photo, a Marine machine gun is firing. The headlights of a passing Jeep are recorded. The wavy line is from a flashlight carried by a Marine as he runs for cover. The bright burst of light at the lower right is from a motion picture projector showing a movie just prior to the attack. This incredible picture was made by SSgt. William G. Wilson, USMC, a combat cameraman with the 2nd Marine Air Wing. The photo was published in over 500 newspapers. (*NARA*)

US troops and an M4 Sherman Dozer C14 attacking Japanese positions on Peleliu. (*NARA*)

Marines in action on Suicide Ridge. (*NARA*)

A US Marine Corps LVT-4 flame thrower in action on Peleliu. (*NARA*)

A 1st Marine Division M9 Bazooka team on Peleliu. (*NARA*)

men of the Army RCT321 arrive on Peleliu to relieve Chesty Puller's 1st Marines. The pontoon causeway had been constructed by Navy Seabees as soon as the beach head had been secured; the causeway stretched from the beach out to the barrier reef

Long before the fighting for Peleliu was over, Navy Seabees got to work repairing the airstrip. The airstrip was in use by Marine aircraft for a considerable time before the island was declared secure.

Men of the 7th or 5th Marines move up to take their turn assaulting the 500 plus caves and tunnels in the Umurbrogol pocket

Caught out in the open, these Japanese were attempting to move one of their artillery pieces when intercepted by Marine aircraft

The text book assault on Ngesebus Island, watched by senior Marine, Army and Navy officers at the invitation of General Rupertus. Here Amtanks, LVT A(1)s and LVT A(4)s precede the troop-carrying Amtracs crossing the narrow stretch of water between Peleliu and Ngesebus on 28 September

Intersection of the East and West roads running left and right of the Umurbrogol mountain. Once in US hands the Umurbrogol became a surrounded pocket but still deadly

Amtank crews check over a severely damaged Japanese landing craft which had been intercepted by US Navy patrols whilst attempting to land reinforcements on the North of Peleliu from Koror

Marines use improvised "Molatov Cocktails" to try and burn out Japanese defenders in the nightmare of the Umurbrogol. Note also Marine at right with grenade launcher attached to his M1 Garand rifle

LVT4 Amtrac
fitted with a Navy
Mk1 flamethrower
(there were 6
such Amtracs on
Peleliu) assaults one
of the estimated
500 caves in the
Umurbrogol

During the night of
27 September (D
+ 12) one of the
8th Marines Gun
Ballation 155mm
guns was moved
up to support 2/5
close in to the
Amiangal Ridge in
the north of Peleliu

Practically nowhere on Peleliu could the Marines dig in. The best they could do for cover was behind blasted trees or pile coral rocks around themselves

Umurbrogol Mountains, the pre-invasion bombardment and constant shelling and bombing stripped the vegetation from the mountains, revealing a nightmare of coral ridges, gullies and sinkholes as well as more than 500 cave emplacements the Japanese had built

Typical landscape that was the Umurbrogol mountains. Coral made it impossible to dig foxholes for cover, at best cover was only possible by stacking rocks and shattered trees

Aerial view of the Umurbrogol mountains, Peleliu. Constant bombing has stripped the numerous ridges, valleys and sinkholes of covering vegetation. At top and bottom can be seen the West and East roads that ran the full length of the Umurbrogol

Men of the 7th Marines move up to relieve "Chesty" Puller's 1st Marines. Puller's 1st Marines were almost decimated in efforts to "maintain momentum" as General Rupertus put it. Eventually Puller's 1st Marines were pulled out of the front line and returned to Pavuvu by the direct orders of General Geiger.

Marine artillery men haul a 75mm Pack howitzer up onto one of the many Umurbrogol ridges

Fully waterproofed M4 Sherman tanks preceded by a "tank dozer" prepare to cross the shallow waters between Peleliu and Ngesebus island in the north of Peleliu. The wooden causeway connecting Peleliu and Ngesebus partially destroyed is in the background

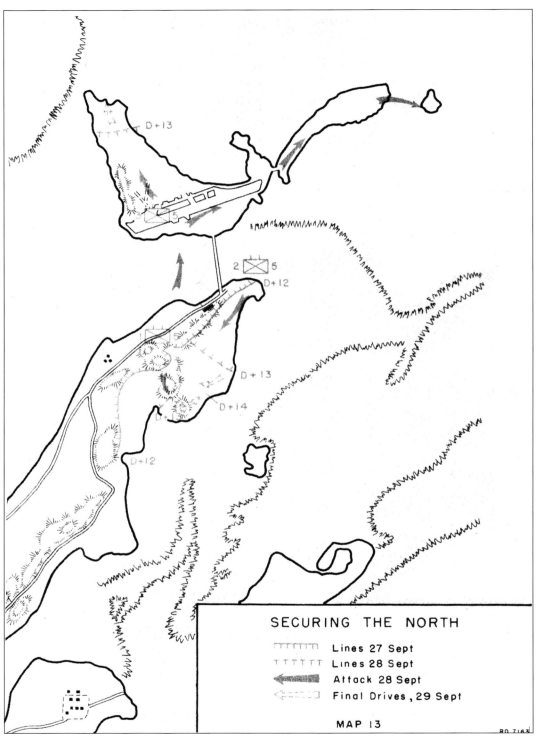

SECURING THE NORTH

	Lines 27 Sept
	Lines 28 Sept
	Attack 28 Sept
	Final Drives, 29 Sept

MAP 13

RO 7163

Securing the North — Peleliu

Getting the wounded out of the Umurbrogol was no easy task. Note rifle grenade on M1 Garand rifle in the foreground, a useful weapon against the many cave defences

Japanese 150mm mortar wreaked havoc among the US forces on Peleliu. There were several of these mortars well dug in among the caves and ridges of the Umurbrogol

Beaches secured, much needed supplies could land. Note the disabled LVTA-4 Amtanks

Colonel Harry D "Bucky" Harris, Commander 5th Marines, confers with General Rupertus, 1st Marine Division, Commander and General Roy Geiger, Commander III AC, prior to 5th Marines operations in the north of Peleliu. It was to Harris that Rupertus offered to hand command of the 1st Marine Division at one low point in the battle

C-46 Commando transport
planes were kitted out with
stretcher racks to transport
the wounded from Peleliu

A Sherman tank leads infantry
up the east road still under fire
from Japanese snipers

Typical terrain of the Umurbrogol Pocket; here one Marine tosses hand grenades at a Japanese cave whilst other Marines provide covering fire

Marine 105mm Howitzers provide artillery support along with Sherman tanks (at right) for the assault of yet another ridge in the Umurbrogol Pocket

Transported to the front in DUKWs, 5th Marines prepare to move North

The northern tip of Peleliu, Ngesebus island in the background

Purple Beach tent city, 1st Marines as they await transports to take them back to Pavuvu

Japanese radar captured almost intact in the north of Peleliu

Chapter Seven

The Nightmare Ends –
The Pocket D+15 – D+32

The Americans now held all apart from the Umurbrogol mountains and were now about to take on the assault of the Japanese defences in the Umurbrogol pocket, an assault which would be reminiscent of siege warfare.

Attacks from the north by 2/321 and 3/321 completed the circle around the Pocket, the 7th Marines pushing from the south and west. 321's attack had until now been held up by Hill B, but this was overcome on D+11 and 321 were able to continue their assault on the Pocket from the north. Although progress was limited, it allowed the Americans to secure their hold on the north side.

On D+14 the 7th Marines received orders to relieve 2/321 and 3/321 in the north. The 1st Division, in order to release 2/7 and 3/7 from holding positions to the west of the Pocket, took hundreds of non-infantry from the supporting artillery, engineers and pioneers units, forming them into composite "Infantillery" units under the command of Lt Colonel Richard B Evans, 11th Marines. The 321st units were relieved by 1/7 and 3/7 on D+14 and continued their assault southwards on D+15, partially taking Boyd Ridge and its southern extension Hill 100 – sometimes known as Popes Ridge or Walt Ridge – although there were still Japanese defenders in the caves of the western slopes.

On D+18 3/5 were back from Ngesebus and reinforced the 7th Marines, who now set about planning a four battalion attack from the north and south. 1/7 and 3/7 would attack from the north, with 2/7 from the south and 3/5 carrying out a diversionary attack on the west into Horseshoe Canyon and Five Sisters. The intense fighting during the attack caused heavy casualties and was only partly successful. Despite 3/5 scaling four of the five ridges of Five Sisters, their position became untenable and they were forced to abandon their gains so far. The assault of Five Sisters was attempted again on the following day but was no more successful.

The 7th Marines had now been in the Umurbrogol for two weeks, their four battalions – including 3/5 – now almost at company strength rather than battalion. At General Geiger's suggestion, General Rupertus relieved the 7th Marines, although being determined that Marines take the Pocket he now turned to the 5th Marines, his only remaining regiment.

The arrival of the 5th Marines would introduce two new concepts to the assault of the Pocket.

First – the attack would be from the north only, which presented the opportunity to take the ridges one at a time.

Second –aerial reconnaissance carried out during the first week on Peleliu had shown Colonel Harris how daunting the Umurbrogol would be, suggesting that only siege tactics would work. He declared his intention to "be lavish with ammunition and stingy with men's lives".

These two philosophies would be applied and remain in place for the duration of the battle.

3/7 were relieved on D+20 by 2/5, who carried out only reconnoitre. Bulldozers cleared the entrances to numerous canyons to the north and prepared the way for flamethrower-mounted LVTs and tanks to be used. Artillery was positioned on the west road, giving point blank fire into the west facing cliffs.

On D+22 tanks went into the Horseshoe, purely to bombard previously identified targets and withdraw.

Following six days of employing these tactics, the Pocket was slowly reduced. Hill 140, the last position, allowed access for a 75mm pack howitzer which was manhandled and sandbagged in place, the sand having been hauled up from the beaches, and was able to fire straight into the mouths of the large caves and provide relief from the murderous fire from one of them which was being rained down on the advancing troops.

3/5 was called in on D+27 to relieve 2/5 but they suffered losses as a result of sniper fire and counter attacks from Nakagawa's men and were only able to complete the relief by D+28. They now took over where 2/5 left off and continued the push from the north using the siege tactics. The remaining men of 1/7 implemented a similar push from the south and between them they reduced the Pocket to an area around 800 yards long by 500 yards wide. Nakagawa reported by radio message to Koror that he had now less than 700 effective troops.

Rupertus was adamant that the Pocket could be taken solely by his Marines, once again refusing assistance from Meuller's 81st Infantry and insisting that his Marines would "very shortly" take the Pocket when General Geiger suggested that 321RCT should relieve the 5th and 7th Marines. Rupertus would be disappointed however as events overtook him. The 81st missing RCT – 323rd – arrived from Ulithi and a message was received from Admiral Nimitz declaring that Peleliu had been secured. General Geiger was ordered to relieve the 1st Marine Division and hand over the islands to 81st infantry for mop up and garrison, the 1st Marine Division then returning to Pavuvu. Tactical operations would remain within the 1st Marine Division's command until that of the 81st Division arrived from Angaur.

During D+31 and D+32 the 5th Marines were relieved by 321RCT. 1/7 still battled in the Pocket until 1/323 relieved them after their arrival from Ulithi on D+32.

On D+35 General Mueller arrived to take over the command of the final reduction of the Pocket, which took RCT322 and 323, plus 2/321, almost six weeks, still using the siege tactics employed by the Marines.

Colonel Nakagawa's final message to his higher-ups on Koror, sent on D+70, advised them that the 2nd Infantry Regiment's colours had been burned and his last remaining 56 men had been divided into 17 groups and ordered to "attack the enemy everywhere".

In the night of D+70/71, 25 Japanese were killed whilst attempting to infiltrate. One of those captured confirmed on the following morning that Colonel Nakagawa and Major General Murai had both committed ritual suicide in the command post.

On the morning of D+73 – 27 November – units from the north and south met face-to-face, at a location which would later be identified as Nakagawa's last command post. Colonel Arthur Watson, 323's commander, reported to General Mueller that the operation was over.

Individual and small groups of Japanese would, however, turn up at times for several years following the operation, the last group consisting of 1 officer and 32 men surrendering in March 1947. The last survivor of the Japanese forces, a Korean labourer, gave himself up in 1954!

Tanks and infantry assault Japanese positions on a Peleliu ridge, 7 October 1944. This is the Horsehoe at it appeared during the later stages: Five Brothers is on the left, Walt Ridge on the right, and Hill 140 in centre background. (*Library of Congress*)

Battle of Peleliu, September–November 1944. A single washing machine, the first to be brought ashore on this recently captured island, does overtime duty at a Second Marine Air Wing encampment. (*National Museum of the US Navy*)

Looking across the coral reefs at two LSTs that were beached on Peleliu. Picture taken in October 1944. (*National Museum of the US Navy*)

Tanks and infantry of the 81st Infantry Division advance in the "Horseshoe" in the Umurbrogol pocket. In the right foreground is the "Freshwater Pond" (only source of water to Japanese Defenders). To the left is "Five Brothers", Hill 140 in the centre background and "Walt Ridge" is on the right.

Peleliu, West Road. Once in US hands it allowed the US to advance northwards, bypassing to Umurbrogol pocket. The West Road was constantly under Japanese sniper fire throughout the campaign

Caves, natural and man-made by the Japanese, covered the Umurbrogol. Over 500 emplacements that had to be taken one by one at great cost to the Marines and soldiers.

Marine Corsairs drop napalm onto Japanese cave defences in the Umurbrogol pocket. Taking off from the captured airfield to the South of Peleliu the Marine planes rarely had time to retract their undercarriage before returning to reload.

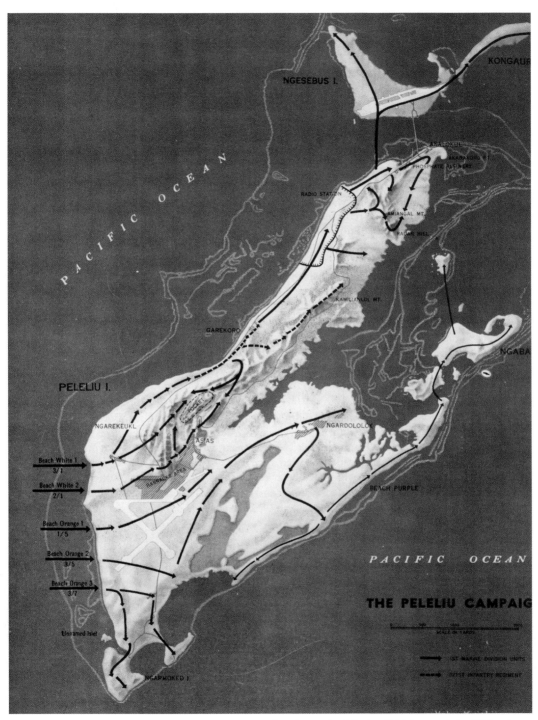

The Peleliu Campaign, showing the advancement of both the 1st Marine Division and the 321st Army Infantry

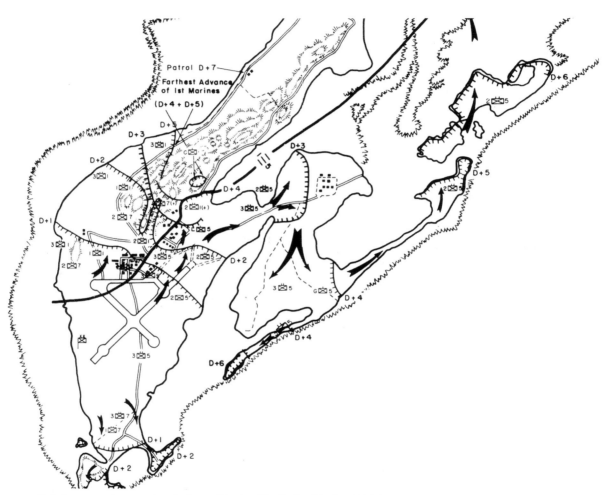

Peleliu, second operational phase (D+1 – D+8). 1st Marine Division

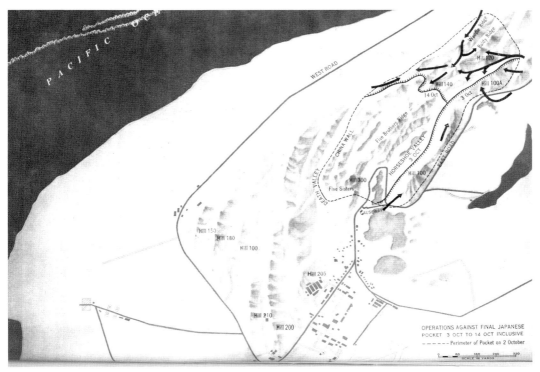

Operations against the Umurbrogol Pocket 3–14 October,

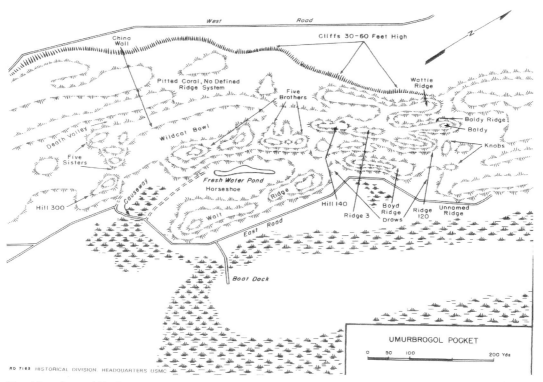

The Umurbrogol Pocket

The Seabees soon had the Peleliu airstrip operational and manned by the Marine Second Air Wing. Bombing missions from the airstrip to the Umurbrogols (in the distance) was thought to be the shortest bombing run in the Pacific war.

Corsair fighters and Curtis C-46 "Commando" transport planes were soon operating out of the Peleliu airstrip

The Umurbrogol Pocket – over 500 caves had been turned into strongholds by the Japanese, each one had to be taken individually

Maj Gen Paul J Mueller (US Army Commanding General 81st Infantry Div) escorts Admiral Halsey (centre) and Marine Maj Gen Geiger (left). Most of Peleliu was in US hands, except the Umurbrogol Pocket, by this time.

The Marine 2nd Air Wing soon had the Peleliu airstrip looking a bit like home, including the New York '21 club'. It was very different for the soldiers and Marines on the front line. Souvenir hunters from the airbase, if they wandered into the front lines, were given a rifle and a taste of war for the infantry!

Chapter Eight

Aftermath

Now that the operation was complete, there was time for reflection and evaluation of the human cost. The 1st Marine Division suffered 6,526 casualties, 1,252 of these killed in action (KIA). The 81st Infantry suffered 1,393 casualties on Peleliu and 1,676 on Angaur. Japanese casualties were estimated to be 10,900, all of which were KIA. Two hundred and two prisoners were taken, of which only 19 were combat troops and the remainder Korean labourers.

The American military were puzzled by one aspect of the battle for Peleliu and that was the role of Major General Murai. Both official orders, captured following the battle, and information gained from interrogation of prisoners, pointed to the fact that Colonel Nakagawa was the island commander and that General Murai was an advisor. This appears strange when one considers the strict Japanese military code and the fact that the garrison on Peleliu far exceeded the usual command level of a Colonel.

General Inoue survived the war and was imprisoned in a US Navy prison in Guam, where he was interviewed in March 1950 by Lt Colonel Worden, USMC. His testimony, in addition to a report from the Japanese Ministry of Foreign Affairs, confirmed that General Murai was on Peleliu during the battle and that he and Colonel Nakagawa both received special promotion to Lieutenant General on 31 December 1944. This was also the date on which the Japanese high command officially accepted the death of both.

Units of the 81st Infantry (RCT321), Navy Seabee and Marine aviation units together garrisoned Peleliu for the next few months. The fighting was over and Peleliu declared secure, but some Japanese remained on the island in isolated pockets and caves, mainly in the north and in the Umurbrogol mountains. These were flushed out by the garrison troops and the caves sealed. Even three months after the fighting in the Umurbrogol pocket, the enormous cave which had been occupied by Japanese Naval Construction Units still contained a handful of Japanese Navy and Army troops. The Americans tried in vain to persuade them to surrender but, having failed, they blasted closed the entrances. Amazingly, in February 1945, five of them dug their way to the surface, only to be captured.

Marine aircraft had started to arrive just after D-day on Peleliu; VMP(N)-541, VMF-114, VMF-121, VMF-122, VMTB-134 and VMR-952. The VMF(N)-541 night fighter squadron had provided support to Marine troops on the ground and, after Peleliu had been secured, on Yap and Babelthuap.

Two Navy sea search units also remained on Peleliu following the battle; patrols from these would later locate survivors from the USS Indianapolis. This vessel had been involved in delivering elements of the atomic bomb to Tinian and on leaving Guam headed for Leyte had been sunk by Japanese submarine I-58. Sadly many survivors had been attacked and eaten by sharks.

In a totally unexpected incident, Japanese troops landed on Purple and White beaches on 18 January 1945 and were challenged by the garrison forces, leaving 71 Japanese dead and two captured.

Remaining elements of the 321st were relieved on 8 February by the Army's 111th Infantry Regiment, who then took over the garrison duties on both Peleliu and Angaur for the remainder of the war.

For many years following the war, rumours abounded regarding surviving Japanese soldiers being in hiding in the mountains and swamps of Peleliu and in fact a Marine regiment was sent out to search for the survivors, who were said to be harassing the local people. There were indications that men were hiding in the mountains and several attempts were made to persuade them to surrender. When all attempts failed, a Japanese Admiral was sent to Peleliu to convince them that the war was over and that they could now surrender with honour. Eventually 26 bedraggled soldiers and sailors and a Lieutenant emerged, finally giving up on their battle for Peleliu.

The Navy Seabees occupied Angaur and commenced work on a 2,250 foot runway and airstrip, which had been started before the island had been secured. From this runway Marine airwings had initially flown sorties to support the battle on Peleliu, but it was manned later by the 494th Heavy Bomb group who flew B24 Liberators in support of US troops fighting the Japanese in the Philippines and against the islands of Koror and Babelthuap, still occupied by General Inoue and several thousand Japanese troops.

As for the 1st Marine Division's Commanders, General Rupertus was relieved of command and given command of the Marine Corps School in the US. He was awarded the Distinguished Service Medal, many believe as a 'sweetener'. He died of a heart attack at Washington Navy Yard on 24 March 1945. Colonels Puller, Harris and Hanneken all returned to the US for a long-overdue rest; in fact the atomic bombs were dropped on Hiroshima and Nagasaki before they received their next commands.

The contrasting approaches to battle between Army and Marine units was one of the notable points to emerge from Peleliu. Whereas the Army preferred superior firepower of artillery and aircraft to reduce defences, thereby reducing the length of battle and number of lives at risk, the Marine approach was for a short but frequently costly campaign in terms of casualties. Criticism was voiced both ways; the Army of the Marines' willingness to risk lives and the Marines of the Army's inability to maintain the momentum of battle. This would become a recurring argument where both Army and Marine units were engaged in the same campaign.

The need to take Peleliu has been the subject of much debate by Generals and historians, but the basic facts remain. Although it raises the question of whether any danger ever existed, MacArthur's flank was now secure for his safe return to the Philippines without any fear or Japanese air strikes or troop reinforcements from the Palaus. Many thousands of first class Japanese troops were eliminated, leaving the remaining troops in the Carolinas easily contained by operations from the new American air bases on Peleliu and Angaur. Also the change of tactics by the Japanese was a useful indication to the Allies of what they could expect in future operations on the Japanese homeland.

View looking south, 29 June 1945, after Peleliu landings in September 1944, the "white" and "orange" landing beaches were on the shoreline at right. (*USNHHC*)

Battle of Peleliu, September–November 1944. A Marine honor guard, aboard a Coast Guard transport gives a body to the sea during burial services for men killed on Peleliu Island in Palau group. The Chaplain and a Coast Guard Commander are standing in the foreground near the two bodies still to be committed. (*National Museum of the US Navy*)

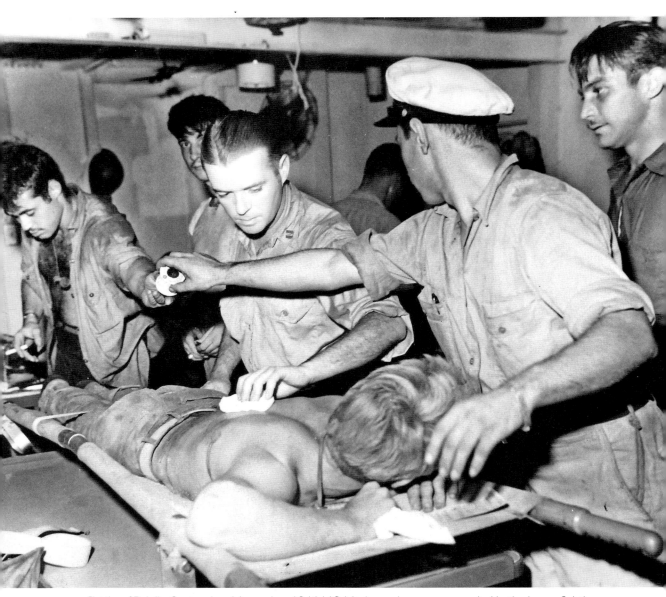

Battle of Peleliu, September–November 1944. U.S. Marines who were wounded in the heavy fighting on Peleliu Islands in the Palau group are transferred to Coast Guard manned transports for hospitalization. Shown: In the chief petty officer's quarters of the ship, converted temporarily into a hospital ward, CPM Neil Dushan, USCG, and Lieutenant W. J. Peilly, care for a wounded man. (*National Museum of the US Navy*)

The Stars and Stripes Over Another Jap Island–Old Glory is raised on a makeshift flagpole atop a crude Japanese observation tower on Peleliu. This was the first formal flag-raising on Peleliu. (*USMC Archives*)

Photographers of the 1st Marine Division who participated in the Peleliu Operation. (*NARA*)

Very few Japanese troops surrendered on Peleliu, choosing to die rather than being captured. Most of the prisoners taken were Korean forced labour troops

Post-war monument to the US Army 81st "Wildcat" Division, 323rd Infantry, on Peleliu

Monument to the 81st Infantry Division (Wildcats) US Army, erected after the war's end atop of the Umurbrogol mountain. Monument still stands today but now foliage has reclaimed the Umurbrogol.

Memorial to the 1st Marine Division (Reinforced), erected after the Second World War and still stands on Peleliu today

Company A, 1st Battalion, 7th Marines. 94 survivors out of the 235 men that landed on Peleliu on D-Day (Charles H Owen)

Dead Marines laid on stretchers and covered with ponchos await burial on Peleliu. Japanese dead were not as fortunate, being left where they fell.

The American cemetery on Peleliu at the dedication in 1944. After the war's end the remains of the fallen were returned to the US for private burial or internment in the Pacific War cemetery on Hawaii. The obelisk still stands atop Bloody Nose Ridge, Peleliu, today.

Inside of one of the 500+ caves used by the Japanese defenders. Most caves were mutually defended, many inter-connected with multiple entrances

Inside a huge cave kitted out as a field hospital by the Japanese. These caves had to be taken by the Americans one by one, with explosives and flamethrowers.

Landing beaches for the 3rd Battalion, 5th Marines, on Ngesebus island to the north of Peleliu. Fiercely defended by the Japanese but soon secured by the Marines. In the distance is Kongauru island, also taken by the Marines.

Well concealed Japanese mortar position on Ngesebus island, only taken out by flamethrowers and demolition charges.

Japanese coastal defence gun taken out by naval gunfire early in the battle. Such guns wreaked havoc on the Amtracs and DUKWs on D-Day.

With the heat and humidity (daytime temperatures reaching 115 degrees F) the dead had to be buried quickly. Here one of many mass graves for the Marines. The Japanese dead were not treated with the same respect but left to rot or sealed in caves where they died.

Aerial view of the Peleliu airstrip now in US hands, the Umurbrogol mountains in the distance now stripped of all vegetation by repeated naval and artillery shelling as well as aerial bombing by aircraft operating from Angaur as well as Peleliu.

Narrow gauge railway ran through the pre-war Phosphate plant on Peleliu. The plant was totally destroyed by the pre-invasion bombardment

Totally destroyed Phosphate Plant on the north of Peleliu

Chronology

1944

February 1–7	US troops capture Kwajalein and Majora Atolls in the Marshall Islands
February 17/18	US carrier-based planes destroy the Japanese naval base at Truk in the Caroline Islands
February 20	US carrier-based and land-based planes destroy the Japanese base at Rabaul
April 24	Japanese 14th Army arrives on the Palau Islands
	Colonel Nakagawa and 10,500 troops are sent to Peleliu plus 1,400 to Angaur
May 29	Operation Stalemate ordered by Admiral Nimitz, Commander-in-Chief, pacific Ocean Areas (CICPOA)
June 19	The "Marianas Turkey Shoot" occurs as US carrier-based fighters shoot down 220
	Japanese planes while only 20 American planes are lost
July 7	Operation Stalemate II – the revised plan for the invasion of the Palau Islands – is issued
July 19	US Marines invade Guam in the Marianas
July 24	US Marines invade Tinian
August 8	American troops complete the capture of the Mariana Islands
August 27 & 29	1st Marine Division conduct practice landings for Peleliu in the Tassafaronga region of Guadalcanal
September 4	Task force leaves Guadalcanal and heads for Peleliu
September 13	Admiral Halsey recommends the cancellation of Stalemate II but is told it is too late to cancel the invasion of Peleliu
September 15	US troops invade Morotai and the Palaus island of Peleliu
September 17	81st Infantry invade Angaur, south of Peleliu
September 21	Angaur declared secure, 81st Infantry available for re-deployment to Peleliu
September 22	81st Infantry units begin to replace 1st Marines on Peleliu
October 15	81st Infantry take over from 1st Marine Division on Peleliu
October 20	US Sixth Army invades Leyte in the Philippines

October 23–26	Battle of Leyte Gulf results in a decisive US naval victory
November 27	81st Infantry declare Peleliu secured
December 15	US troops invade Mindoro in the Philippines

1947

April 21	Lt Yamaguchi and 26 men surrender on Peleliu

1954 Lone Korean labourer is the last man to surrender on Peleliu

Tom Lea Paintings

Tom Lea, Time Life magazine correspondent and war artist, landed on Orange Beach 3 with the 7th Marines. His sketches and painting graphically show the horror of war. Probably his best known being the 'Two Thousand Yard Stare' (see Plate 4)

Going In – First Wave

For an hour we plowed toward the beach, the sun above us coming down through the overcast like a silver burning ball…. Over the gunwale of a craft abreast of us I saw a Marine, his face painted for the jungle, his eyes set for the beach, his mouth set for murder, his big hands quiet now in the last moments before the tough tendons drew up to kill. *Caption by the artist, Tom Lea*

The Beach…. My First View as I came around from the ramp of our LVT

We ground to a stop, after a thousand years, on the coarse coral …. And we ran down the ramp and came around the end of the LCT, splashing ankle-deep up the surf to the white beach. Suddenly I was completely alone. Each man drew into himself when he ran down that ramp, into that flame. Those Marines flattened in the sand on that beach were dark and huddled like wet rats in death as I threw my body down among them". *Caption by the artist, Tom Lea*

The Blockhouse

Looking up at the head of the trail I could see the big Jap blockhouse that commanded the height. The thing was now a great jagged lump of concrete, smoking. I saw our lead man meet a front line detail posted by the blockhouse while the other troops advanced down the hill with the three tanks and the flamethrowers. Isolated Jap snipers were at work on our slope, small groups of Marines fanned out on both sides of the trail to clean them out, while we climbed toward the blockhouse.

Caption by the artist, Tom Lea

Down from Bloody Ridge too late. He's finished – Washed up – Gone

As we passed sick bay, still in the shell hole, it was crowded with wounded, and somehow hushed in the evening light. I noticed a tattered Marine standing quietly by a corpsman, staring stiffly at nothing. His mind had crumbled in battle, his jaw hung, and his eyes were like two black empty holes in his head"

Caption by the artist, Tom Lea

The Price

Lying there in terror looking longingly up the slop to better cover, I saw a wounded man near me, staggering in the direction of the LVTs. His face was half bloody pulp and the mangled shreds of what was left of an arm hung down like a stick, as he bent over in his stumbling, shock-crazy walk. The half of his face that was still human had the most terrifying look of abject patience I have ever seen. He fell behind me, in a red puddle on the white sand. *Caption by the artist, Tom Lea*

Sick Bay in a Shellhole – The Padre read: 'I am the Resurrection and the Light'
About thirty paces back of the jap trench a sick bay had been established in a big shell crater made by one of our battleship guns …. In the center of the crater at the bottom a doctor was working on the worst of the stretcher cases. Corpsmen, four to a stretcher, came in continually with their bloody loads ….The padre stood by with two canteens and a Bible, helping. He was deeply and visibly moved by the patient suffering and death. He looked very lonely, very close to God, as he bent over the shattered men so far from home." *Caption by the artist, Tom Lea*

This is Sad Sack calling Charlie Blue

We found the battalion commander [Lt Col Edward H Hurst, CO, 3/7] sitting on a smashed wet log in the mud, marking positions on his map. By him sat his radioman, trying to make contact with company commands on the portable set propped up in the mud. There was an infinitely tired and plaintive patience in the radioman's voice as he called code names, repeating time and again 'This is Sad Sack calling Charlie…'" *Caption by the artist, Tom Lea*

Counterattack

The phone rang. A battalion CO reported the Japs' infiltration and the beginning of the counterattack. He asked what reserves were available and was told there were none. Small arms fire ahead of us became a continuous rattle. Abruptly three star shells burst in the sky. As soon as they died floating down, others flared to take their place. Then the howitzers just behind us opened up, hurling their charges over our heads, shaking the ground with their blasts. *Caption by the artist, Tom Lea*

Appendix I

8 Medal Of Honor Recipients, 1st Marine Division, Peleliu

For conspicuous gallantry and intrepidity at the risk of his life above and beyond the call of duty . . .

First Lieutenant Carlton R. Rouh

CITATION: For conspicuous gallantry and intrepidity at the risk of his life above and beyond the call of duty while attached to the First Battalion, Fifth Marines, First Marine Division, during action against enemy Japanese forces on Peleliu Island, Palau Group, 15 September 1944. Before permitting his men to use an enemy dugout as a position for an 81-mm. Mortar Observation Post, First Lieutenant Rouh made a personal reconnaissance of the pillbox and, upon entering, was severely wounded by Japanese rifle fire from within. Emerging from the dugout, he was immediately assisted by two Marines to a less exposed area but, while receiving first aid, was further endangered by an enemy grenade which was thrown into their midst. Quick to act in spite of his weakened condition, he lurched to a crouching position and thrust both men aside, placing his own body between them and the grenade and taking the full blast of the explosion himself. His exceptional spirit of loyalty and self-sacrifice in the face of almost certain death reflects the highest credit upon First Lieutenant Rouh and the United States Naval Service.

FRANKLIN D. ROOSEVELT

Corporal Lewis K. Bausell

CITATION: For conspicuous gallantry and intrepidity at the risk of his life above and beyond the call of duty while serving with the First Battalion, Fifth Marines, First Marine Division, during action against enemy Japanese forces on Peleliu Island, Palau Group, 15 September 1944. Valiantly placing himself at the head of his squad, Corporal Bausell led the charge forward against a hostile pillbox which was covering a vital sector of the beach and, as the first to reach the emplacement, immediately started firing his automatic into the aperture while the remainder of his men closed in on the enemy. Swift to act as a Japanese grenade was hurled into their midst, Corporal Bausell threw himself on the deadly weapon, taking the full blast of the explosion and sacrificing his own life to save his men. His unwavering loyalty and inspiring courage reflect the highest credit upon Corporal Bausell and the United States Naval Service. He gallantly gave his life for his country.

FRANKLIN D. ROOSEVELT

Pfc. (later 2d Lt.) Arthur J. Jackson

CITATION: For conspicuous gallantry and intrepidity at the risk of his life above and beyond the call of duty, while serving with the Third Battalion, Seventh Marines, First Marine Division, in action against enemy Japanese forces on the Island of Peleliu in the Palau Group, 18 September 1944. Boldly taking the initiative when his platoon's left-flank advance was held up by the fire of Japanese troops concealed in strongly fortified positions, Private First Class Jackson unhesitatingly proceeded forward of our lines and, courageously defying the heavy barrages, charged a large pillbox housing approximately thirty-five enemy soldiers. Pouring his automatic fire into the opening of the fixed installation to trap the occupying troops, he hurled white phosphorus grenades and explosive charges brought up by a fellow Marine, demolishing the pillbox and killing all of the enemy. Advancing alone under the continuous fire from other hostile emplacements, he employed similar means to smash two smaller positions in the immediate vicinity. Determined to crush the entire pocket of resistance although harassed on all sides by the shattering blasts of Japanese weapons and covered only by small rifle parties, he stormed one gun position after another, dealing death and destruction to the savagely fighting enemy in his inexorable drive against the remaining defenses and succeeded in wiping out a total of twelve pillboxes and fifty Japanese soldiers. Stout-hearted and indomitable despite the terrific odds, Private First Class Jackson resolutely maintained control of the platoon's left-flank movement throughout his valiant one-man assault and, by his cool decision and relentless fighting spirit during a critical situation, contributed essentially to the complete annihilation of the enemy in the southern sector of the island. His gallant initiative and heroic conduct in the face of extreme peril reflect the highest credit upon Private First Class Jackson and the United States Naval Service.

HARRY S. TRUMAN

Private First Class Richard E. Kraus

CITATION: For conspicuous gallantry and intrepidity at the risk of his life above and beyond the call of duty while serving with the Eighth Amphibian Tractor Battalion, Third Amphibious Corps, Fleet Marine Force, in action against enemy Japanese forces on Peleliu, Palau Islands, on 3 October 1944. Unhesitatingly volunteering for the extremely hazardous mission of evacuating a wounded comrade from the front lines, Private First Class Kraus and three companions courageously made their way forward and successfully penetrated the lines for some distance before the enemy opened with an intense, devastating barrage of hand grenades which forced the stretcher party to take cover and subsequently abandon the mission. While returning to the rear, they observed two men approaching who appeared to be Marines and immediately demanded the password. When, instead of answering, one of the two Japanese threw a hand grenade into the midst of the group, Private First Class Kraus heroically flung himself upon the grenade and, covering it with his body, absorbed the full impact of the explosion and was instantly killed. By his prompt action and great personal valor in the face of almost certain death, he saved the lives of his three companions, and his loyal spirit of self-sacrifice reflects the highest credit upon himself and the United States Naval Service. He gallantly gave his life for his comrades.

HARRY S. TRUMAN

Private First Class John D. New

CITATION: For conspicuous gallantry and intrepidity at the risk of his own life above and beyond the call of duty while serving with the Second Battalion, Seventh Marines, First Marine Division, in action against enemy Japanese forces on Peleliu Island, Palau Group, 25 September 1944. When a Japanese soldier emerged from a cave in a cliff directly below an observation post and suddenly hurled a grenade into the position from which two of our men were directing mortar fire against enemy emplacements, Private First Class New instantly perceived the dire peril to the other Marines and, with utter disregard for his own safety, unhesitatingly flung himself upon the grenade and absorbed the full impact of the explosion, thus saving the lives of the two observers. Private First Class New's great personal valor and selfless conduct in the face of almost certain death reflect the highest credit upon himself and the United States Naval Service. He gallantly gave his life for his country.

FRANKLIN D. ROOSEVELT

Private First Class Wesley Phelps

CITATION: For conspicuous gallantry and intrepidity at the risk of his life above and beyond the call of duty while serving with the Third Battalion, Seventh Marines, First Marine Division, in action against enemy Japanese forces on Peleliu Island, Palau Group, during a savage hostile counterattack on the night of 4 October 1944. Stationed with another Marine in an advanced position when a Japanese hand grenade landed in his foxhole, Private First Class Phelps instantly shouted a warning to his comrade and rolled over on the deadly bomb, absorbing with his own body the full, shattering impact of the exploding charge. Courageous and indomitable, Private First Class Phelps fearlessly gave his life that another might be spared serious injury and his great valor and heroic devotion to duty in the face of certain death reflected the highest credit upon himself and the United States Naval Service. He gallantly gave his life for his country.

HARRY S. TRUMAN

Captain Everett P. Pope

CITATION: For conspicuous gallantry and intrepidity at the risk of his life above and beyond the call of duty while serving as Commanding Officer of Company C, First Battalion, First Marines, First Marine Division, during action against enemy Japanese forces on Peleliu Island, Palau Group, on 19-20 September 1944. Subjected to point-blank cannon fire which caused heavy casualties and badly disorganized his company while assaulting a steep coral hill, Captain Pope rallied his men and gallantly led them to the summit in the face of machine-gun, mortar and sniper fire. Forced by wide-spread hostile attack to deploy the remnants of his company thinly in order to hold the ground won, and with his machine guns out of action and insufficient water and ammunition, he remained on the exposed hill with twelve men and one wounded officer, determined to hold through the night. Attacked continuously with grenades, machine guns and rifles from three sides and twice subjected to suicidal charges during the night, he and his valiant men fiercely beat back or destroyed the enemy, resorting to hand-to-hand combat as the supply of ammunition dwindled and still maintaining his lines with his eight remaining riflemen when daylight brought more deadly fire and he was ordered to withdraw. His valiant leadership against devastating odds while protecting the units below from heavy Japanese attack reflects the highest credit upon Captain Pope and the United States Naval Service.

FRANKLIN D. ROOSEVELT

Private First Class Charles H. Roan

CITATION: For conspicuous gallantry and intrepidity at the risk of his life above and beyond the call of duty while serving with the Second Battalion, Seventh Marines, First Marine Division, in action against enemy Japanese forces on Peleliu, Palau Islands, 18 September 1944. Shortly after his leader ordered a withdrawal upon discovering that the squad was partly cut off from their company as a result of their rapid advance along an exposed ridge during an aggressive attack on the strongly entrenched enemy, Private First Class Roan and his companions were suddenly engaged in a furious exchange of hand grenades with Japanese forces emplaced in a cave on higher ground and to the rear of the squad. Seeking protection with four other Marines in a depression in the rocky, broken terrain, Private First Class Roan was wounded by an enemy grenade which fell close to their position and, immediately realizing the imminent peril to his comrades when another grenade landed in the midst of the group, unhesitatingly flung himself upon it, covering it with his body and absorbing the full impact of the explosion. By his prompt action and selfless conduct in the face of almost certain death, he saved the lives of four men, and his great personal valor reflects the highest credit upon himself and the United States Naval Service. He gallantly gave his life for his comrades.

HARRY S. TRUMAN

Appendix II

Surrender Leaflets Dropped by US Forces on the Remaining Japanese in the Umurbrogol Pocket and Retaliatory Surrender Leaflet from the Japanese Forces to the Americans

Appendices to Annex B to PALAU Operation, Special Action Report.

1. (a)

       Imperial Soldiers:

           An American victory in this battle is assured. Our soldiers admire your courage and skill. However, American superiority in manpower and material makes our eventual triumph inevitable. We dislike to continue the slaughter of brave soldiers like yourselves. Speaking as soldier to soldier we urge you to end this combat.

           When the struggle is over we shall give you the best possible treatment. You shall have food and rest and your wounded will be given the finest medical care available.

           If you walk towards our lines along the Uragai Road between 1200 and 1400 hours tomorrow afternoon holding this paper we shall understand that you are complying with this request.

           Once again we urge you to end this struggle.

帝國ノ軍人

此ノ戰斗ハ米軍ノ勝利デアル事ハ明 カニナッタ。吾々米軍ハ君達ノ勇氣ト戰術ニ大ニ敬馬イタ。感心。併シ我々ハ武器ト立ハ力ノ為メ最後ニ吾等ノ勝利ハウタゼ無イ。我々ハソンナニ勇シク戰ッタ君達ガ皆戰死スル事ハ望マナイ。軍人ト軍人ノ互ノ尊敬上ノ君達ニ此ノ戰斗ヲ止メル事ヲ進メル。

戰斗ヲ止メタ際ハ君達ヲ我等ノ出来ル限リ良ク取扱ッテヤル。我等ハ君達皆ニ食料ト休ソクヲ與ヘル機關ガ充分アル。特ニ怪我人ヤ病人ヲ手當ヲスル機關ガアル。

明日正午十二時頃ヨリ後午二時頃迄近裏街道ヘ此ノ丸ヲ持ッテ出テ来レバ君達ガ此ノ通告ニ應ジルト認ム。

又モ此ノ戰斗ヲ中止スル事ヲ進メル。

Appendices to Annex B to PALAU Operation, Special Action Report.

1.   (b)

Gallant Officers and Men of the Japanese Empire:

For the past 12 days your land, naval, and air forces have tried various means to reinforce you. But because of the great superiority of our forces the greater part of the reinforcements have been sent to the bottom. We have already occupied the airfield and the greater part of the island and are about to launch an all-out attack to wipe out all vestiges of resistance.

Officers and men, you now have the greatest decision of your lives before you. It is indeed heroic to die a glorious death on the battlefield, but is it not your responsibility and duty to rebuild Japan after this war is over? The American forces are willing to give any man who is desirous of abandoning this heroic but futile fight for the greater job of building the future Japan, the opportunity to do so.

Anyone who unarmed and with both hands raised, brings this paper and comes down the URAGAIDO tomorrow, 29 September between 1200 and 1400 will be allowed to pass our front lines and be escorted to the rear where food, water, and clothing are plentiful.

勇敢ナル帝國ノ將兵

去ル十三日間帝國ノ陸海並ニ航空軍ハ色々ナ

方法ヲ取リテ此ノ島ヲ増援セントシタ。併シ米軍ノ

大力機動隊ノ為ニ其ノ大部分ハ海底ニ沈没サシタ。

米軍ハ既ニ此ノ島ノ大部分並ニ飛行場ヲ占領シ

今ニ残ッタ兵力ノ全滅ヲ開始セントスル所デアル。

之ニモ拘ラズ戦斗ヲ勇シク模範的ニ続ケテ居ル

君達ニ感心シタ。帝國ノ將兵、之ハ君達一生ノ

最大ノ判決問題デアル。美事ニ戦死スルハ誠ニ

勇シ。併シ此ノ戦争ガ終ッタ後再ビ日本ヲ健テ上

ゲルハ君達ノ義務デモ責任デハナイカ。武士的ハ玄ヘ

無駄ナ戦死ヲスルヨリ。今カラ勤將来日本ヲ健テカヘル

ト思フ希望者がアレバ米軍ハ其ノ機會ヲアタヘル。

希望者ハ此ノ札ヲ持チ明日九月二十九日正午

十二時頃ヨリ十四時頃迄ニ裏街道ヲ武器ナシニテ

手ヲ上ゲダマゝ来レバ我ガ米軍ハ米軍予一線ノ

通過ヲ許ス亦後方ニ飲食ヤ衣服ノ充分アル

休憩所ヘ御迎ヘル。

九月二十八日

Appendices to Annex B to PALAU Operation, Special Action Report.

1. (c)

Officers of the Japanese forces:

As you can see if you look at the planes, the material and the ships, your best efforts are not impeding our work. American planes not only bomb you at will but they also bomb Babelthuap and the other islands North of here. Perhaps you can see the flames. Your comrades to the North have all they can do to help themselves so how could they help you?

You honor and respect your men, but how can they honor and respect you if you make them die needlessly. Thousands of brave Japanese soldiers before you have realized the futility of death in such circumstances; they will live to raise families and to help build a new Japan.

You still have this choice — raise a white flag and come out unarmed. We will give you water, food, shelter, and medicine for your wounded.

日本ノ將校殿

米側ノ偉大ナル飛行機、武器、又ハ船舶

ヲ見レバ貴殿ノ戦略デハ米軍ノ目的ヲ停止

スル事ハ出来ナイ。米機ハ貴殿ノ陣地ヲ自由

ニ爆撃スルバカリデハナク、パラオ本島、コロール島

又ハ他ノ島々ヲ破壊シテ居ル。今僅カニ其ノ

火焰ヲ見ル事ガ出来マセウ。北地區ノ友軍ハ出来

ル限リ貴隊ヲ援助シヨウト思ッテ居ルケレドモ、

ドウシテモ援スル事ガ出来マセウカ。

貴殿ハ兵隊達ヲ夢ヲ教スルガ多数ノ兵ヲ

無駄ニ犠牲スル事ハ貴殿ノ名譽ヲ傷ツケ

ルバカリデハナイデセウ。勇敢ナル數千ノ日本軍人ハ

無駄ニ戦死スル事ヲ無益ダト認メ闔後歸還

シテ新ニ大日本ヲ建設スル時期ヲ機待シテ居マス。

此ノ機會ヲ求ダ利用スル事ガ出来マス。

米側デハ水、食糧又ハ治療ヲ與ヘツ上貴殿

ニ對シテ便宜ヲ計リマスカラ　白旗ヲ上ゲ武器

ヲ棄テ外出シテ来ナサイ。

Appendices to Annex B to PALAU Operation, Special Action Report.

1.   (d)

    TO: Col. NAKAGAWA

    C.O. Japanese Garrison, Peleliu Island.

    The American forces have met the Japanese Army in Guadalcanal, Bougainville, Saipan, Guam and countless other islands of the Pacific. The Japanese Army has always fought bravely, and, when overwhelmed by numbers, the remnants, consistently refusing to yield, have either taken grave steps to end the situation themselves*, or have died attacking us.

    As neither course has been taken by the forces on Peleliu in this present instance, it is possible that a third solution may be under consideration.

    The American forces therefore are willing to offer honorable treatment to yourself, your officers and men in case such should be requested.

*   T.N.:   That is, they have committed Harakiri.

ペリリュー島守備隊司令官

中川大佐殿

日米大事件開始ニ以来今日迄米軍ハ
猛烈果敢ナル皇軍トガ島、ボ島、サイパン、
大宮島及ビ太平洋ノ諸島デ會戦ニ故ニ
幾ラ米軍ノ兵力ガ多数ニ座例シテモ大
和魂ヲ持ナ得ル勇敢ナ勇士ハ予盾ヲ抵抗
シテ最後ノ突重ヲ行イ勇敢ニ戦死ヲ遂ケテ
オルデハナイカ。
コレニ遁ヒ現在ノ状態ニ依レバ、ペリリュー島
ニ於イテ猛烈ナ大和魂精神ヲ発揮シテ
井ナイガ他ノ解決考慮中デモアレバ米
軍ハ貴殿將校又ハ兵ニ對シテ正當ナ
待遇ヲ當ヘル予定デアル。

米派遣軍司令官

Appendices to Annex B to PALAU Operation, Special Action Report.

2.

American brave soldiers:

We think your much pity since landing on this ileland. In spite of your pitiful battle, we are sorry that we can present only fire, not even good water. We soon will attack strongly your army. You had done bravely your duty.

Now, Abandon your guns, and come in Japanese military with white flag (or handkerchief), so we will be glad to see you and welcome you comfortably as we can well.

American brave soldiers!
We think your much pity since
landing on this island. In
spite of your pitiful battle,
we are sorry that we can present
only fire, not even good water.
We soon will [...] with strong
[...]. You had [...]
[...]

Now, Abandon your guns,
and come in Japanese militar[y]
with white flag (or handkerchief).
We [...] will be glad [...]
[...] you [...]
comfortably as we can will [...]

此ノ札ヲ持ツテ来ル兵ヲ最近ノ
指揮所ヘ傷ツケズ導ケ

The bearer (s) of this ticket
are to be escorted to the nearest
command post unharmed.

Bibliography

Peleliu: Tragic Triumph: The Untold Story of the Pacific War's Forgotten Battle, Bill D Ross, Random House, ISBN 0-394-56588-6 1992

Peleliu 1944, Henry A Gailey, Nautical & Aviation Publishing Inc 1983

The Assault on Peleliu, Major Frank O Hough, US Government Printing Office

The Old Breed, George McMillan, Infantry Journal Press 1949

The Devil's Anvil, The Assault on Peleliu Island, James H Hallas, Praeger Publishers 1944

With the Old Breed at Peleliu and Okinawa, Eugene B Sledge, Presidio Press 1981

Marine! The Life of Lieutenant General Lewis B (Chesty) Puller USMC (Ret), Burke Davis, Little, Brown Company 1962

Coral Comes High, George P Hunt, Harper & Brothers 1946

Western Pacific Operations, Vol 4, History of US Marine Corps Operations in World War II, USMC

To the Far Side of Hell — The Battle for Peleliu 1944, Derrick Wright, The University of Alabama Press Tuscaloosa

HBO Mini Series — "Pacific"